HEALING

HEALING

Stories of Faith, Hope, and Love

Jan Alkire

Paulist Press
New York/Mahwah, N.J.

Cover design by Diego Linares
Book design by Lynn Else

Library of Congress Cataloging-in-Publication Data

Alkire, Jan
    Healing : stories of faith, hope, and love / Jan Alkire.
        p. cm.
    Includes bibliographical references and index.
    ISBN 0-8091-4173-6 (alk. paper)
    1. Spiritual healing. 2. Church work with the sick. 3. Prayer—Catholic Church. I. Title.
    BT732.5 .A43 2003
    234'.131—dc21

                                                                2003006109

Published by Paulist Press
997 Macarthur Boulevard
Mahwah, New Jersey 07430

www.paulistpress.com

Printed and bound in the
United States of America

Contents

CONTENTS

For Fred, with love

Foreword

When the afflicted cry out, the Lord hears them,
and from all their anguish rescues them.
Close is the Lord to the brokenhearted,
and those crushed in spirit he heals. (Ps 34:17–18)

These are beautiful words, but are they true? Is there any evidence that God really cares, that he does heal? I think there is evidence that God heals us, rescues us, watches over us. In Jesus we see God.

Over and over the Gospels say that Jesus was deeply moved by the plight of people who were sick, or grieving the loss of a loved one, or shunned by society. In his healing ministry he showed people that God cared about each and every individual. He didn't wave a magic wand and heal all in Palestine or in the world. Instead, he healed one-by-one—touching, embracing, weeping, encouraging, exhorting. Through him, people came to realize that God loved them as his children, and that God grieved when his children suffered. Jesus gave people hope when things seemed hopeless. He showed them that things could be different. He gave them a future.

Jesus continues doing these things today. He did not quit when he ascended into heaven. Through scripture and community and prayer, Jesus tells us that things can be different. We are not alone. We are not helpless. We are not without hope.

But Jesus always seemed to require people to be active in their own healing. "Stretch out your hand," he said to the man with the shriveled hand. "Pick up your mat and walk," he told the paralytic at the Pool of Bethesda. "Lazarus! Come out!" he called to his dead and entombed friend. So in the days ahead, expect that Jesus will require action from you. Listen for what that will be. Pray that you may know what to do. Pray for readiness.

God wants you to experience Jesus meeting you in your need, to know you have a God who cares.

Leo Thomas, O.P.
1996

Acknowledgments

It takes a village to raise a child, and the same holds true for writing a book: It takes a village. Here are some of the people in my "village" who helped bring this book into existence:

The support of my husband Fred gave me the freedom to write. He has been like St. Joseph, loyal spouse and friend.

Joan Bell, Candy Stickney, Pat King, and Father Jack Murphy, S.J., gave me invaluable feedback, encouragement, and help. Often they were like the angel who brought water and a cake of bread to Elijah to strengthen him for his journey.

Jackie Huetter and countless prayer intercessors prayed me through the past two-and-a-half years. They were a communion of saints journeying at my side.

Betty Dameron was the sister in Christ I turned to whenever I needed a Protestant perspective on what I was writing. She helped me experience the unity of all Christians.

Teri Howatt and a number of other friends tried out various chapters for their own healing, then gave me their reactions. They helped me experience the reality of who would be reading this book.

Many, many people shared hurts and healing stories with me. Their experiences brought this book to life.

Finally, my mentor and longtime coauthor, Father Leo Thomas, O.P., went home to the Lord in 1997, but his influence on me as a writer continues to grow.

These people—and many more—bring to mind words of Saint Paul:

I thank my God every time I remember you, constantly praying with joy in every one of my prayers for all of you, because of your sharing in the gospel from the first day until now. (Phil 1:3–4)

"Is There Hope?"

...I came that they may have life, and have it abundantly.
(John 10:10)

A friend, Meg, phoned to say she was afflicted with an ail-
ment she knew I had wrestled with years earlier. Also, a recent
surgery had gone all wrong—now she was permanently dis-
abled. And food allergies were limiting her life so much that it
felt like being trapped in a dietary wheelchair. After telling me
this in the space of a couple of minutes, Meg said, "I just called
to ask you one question: Is there any hope for me?"

That is the question: Is there hope when suffering enters
your life like an unwelcome guest and seems to become a permanent resident in your body, mind, and/or spirit? Is there
hope when pain goes on for what feels like eternity and
you've tried everything you can imagine to resolve it? Is there
hope when you pray for healing and all you hear in return is
the sound of silence? Is there hope even when there may be
no cure?

When Meg asked her question, she did not need a "sure-
there's-hope" reply. She did not need a scripture quote or unso-
licited advice. Most of all, she did not need to hear "everything
is going to be all right," followed by "good-bye."

Responses like these don't work, of course, because when
suffering leaves you or me feeling lower than a sidewalk curb,

we don't need sound-bites, clichés, quotes, and unasked-for advice. We need hope. Here is what I've discovered about hope and how it relates to this book and, possibly, to your need:

1. *Hope empowers us to journey toward healing.* Meg's lack of hope had reduced her to sitting and staring at a wall. She felt incapable of seeking help. That's because a person without hope is like a car without fuel. The engine won't even turn over. If your need for healing has immobilized you, perhaps you are suffering from a lack of hope.

2. *Hope is a gift from God.* No one could force-feed hope into Meg. She needed to receive it from the Holy Spirit. This book contains a number of step-by-step guides to help you receive an increase of God's gifts, including the gift of hope.

3. *The gift of hope usually comes through the power of community.* Meg needed a diverse community, not isolation. She needed empathy and compassionate help from many resources. Within these pages you will find ideas for how to locate and use a variety of resources.

4. *Hope requires action on our part.* Meg wanted to take part in her own healing, yet didn't know where to turn. The main purpose of this book is to show readers how to actively participate in their own healing. Within these pages you will find stories, descriptions, and tools to help you gain greater health than you now possess.

5. *Hope surrenders to God and to today's reality.* Father Leo Thomas and I explain this in our book *Healing as a Parish Ministry*:

> Hope-filled people see their desperate situation but refuse to believe this is all there is to reality. The virtue of hope says that God is dealing with life in ways that surpass our ability to grasp.[1]

Fatalism? No. A willingness to "let go and let God"? Yes. You probably have concrete ideas as to where you need healing. Through this book, you may discover where God wants to bring you into more wholeness than you can imagine.

6. *Hope says "yes" to a future in which the only guarantee is God's loving presence.* If there were a lemon law for the human body, Meg surely would qualify for a free replacement. Alas, no such law exists. What Meg and you and I get instead is a promise from the Risen Lord: "I am with you always" (Matt 28:20). Beyond that, we get no warranty—a scary thought unless we keep in mind that Jesus also said that he had come to bring us abundant life.

No matter how much fullness of life you have right now, God wants to give you more. If you hurt right now, God wants to soothe your pain. If you don't know where to turn for support right now, God wants to show you choices. I pray that this book will help these things happen. More than that, I pray for you to experience God's soothing, healing presence in the midst of your need. In the words of Saint Paul:

> I ask that your minds may be opened to see God's light, so that you will know what is the hope to which he has called you, how rich are the wonderful blessings he promises his people, and how very great is his power at work in us who believe. This power working in us is the same as the mighty strength which God used when he raised Christ from death. (Eph 1:18–20a GNT)

Looking Ahead

Here are some of the subjects covered in this book:

- The ideal healing.

- Ten resources for healing—medical, psychological, spiritual.

- Healing through types of prayer that are centuries old.

- Healing in the midst of a serious illness.

- The healing journey from Good Friday to Pentecost and beyond.

PART ONE

Getting Started

CHAPTER 1

The Need for Healing

You will know the truth, and the truth will make you free. (John 8:32)

Chris felt tired at a bone-deep level. His daily jogs had become daily slogs. His body felt as though someone had snuck up behind him and strapped exercise weights onto his legs and arms. What was going on?

Actually, Chris preferred not to know what was going on. He favored the ignore-it-and-it-will-go-away approach to healing. Now if only his wife would quit mentioning his need for a physical and his family history of high blood pressure. If only he could talk himself into more energy...

A series of coincidences led to discovery of the truth. On Sunday, Chris read a columnist's vivid description of his recent stroke. On Tuesday a friend told Chris about stroke-like symptoms she was having. On Wednesday a former work colleague phoned to say how crummy his life was as a stroke survivor. On Thursday, a niggling thought began to appear on the computer screen of Chris's mind: Maybe he should check out his blood pressure. The news, when it finally arrived, felt terrible. Chris learned he had a blood pressure of 220/120. Basically, the top of his head was about to blow off.

Jesus told his followers, "You will know the truth and the truth will make you free," but when it comes to a need for healing, it's too bad he didn't add that before the truth makes you free, it may throw you down on the ground and leave you feeling as helpless as a turtle on its back. Perhaps that's why it's human nature to ignore, suppress, repress, stifle, and squelch all thoughts about the need for healing. We avoid the truth because deep down we know a gap exists between knowing it and being set free by it.

An innate wisdom tells us that healing takes time, effort, and yes, some suffering. That's the bad news. The good news is that once a wound or illness is discovered, healing becomes possible. Knowing the truth brings with it the power to do something about it. Once Chris knew about his hypertension, he was able to be treated for it. He spent a rocky three months trying different medications, but eventually one was found that worked well with almost no side effects. Now one pill a day keeps Chris's blood pressure down to 120/80. His energy has returned. He's back to jogging. Life is good.

Four Kinds of Wounds/Illnesses

Unless a wound or illness is minor, it will involve every aspect of our being: physical, emotional, spiritual, and relational. The primary problem may be any one of these.[1]

Physical Wounds

Physical wounds damage the human body: skin, heart, spinal cord, and so on. Arising from injury, disease, or congenital condition, they're easy to describe. Would that all of them were as easy to diagnose and treat as Chris's physical problem—painless blood pressure tests, a pill a day, and clear-cut results. By contrast, pain and misery accompany a number of physical wounds, for example, arthritis, multiple sclerosis, traumatic injuries, cancer. Treatment of these can require great courage and fortitude.

Emotional Wounds

Emotions can be positive (e.g., joy, peacefulness, love) or negative (e.g., fear, anger, resentment, hate, anxiety, depression) and can be appropriate or destructive; healthy or unhealthy.

When Chris discovered his sky-high blood pressure, he responded with sky-high fear as he recalled his grandfather's life after a stroke: slumped in a wheelchair, glassy-eyed, unable to speak, a shadow of his former self, then dead at 65. Would this be his fate too? These thoughts and fears, although negative, were appropriate. Chris was staring at a picture of his family history and its possibilities. What hadn't been healthy was his avoidance of the negative. Denial almost led to the disaster he feared.

Emotions such as worry, resentment, and depression are hurtful, not helpful. They often arise from deprivation or trauma and eventually lead to health problems or to distorted and destructive behavior.

For example, one day a widowed mother put her toddler, David, in his bedroom, stuffed rags at the bottom of the door, went downstairs, and turned on the gas oven. Two daughters found her body when they got home from school. Life then went from bad to brutal for the three children because the uncle who adopted them also sexually abused them for fifteen years.

Flashbacks paralyzed David with anxiety long after his mother's death and uncle's abuse. And migraines triggered by the anxiety flattened him for days at a time. The events were over, but the trauma was not. David needed healing from memories of a past that kept hurting the present.[2]

Memory enables us to know our name, to retain knowledge, and to grow in grace and wisdom. But every coin has two sides, including the coin of memory. It is here where our emotional wounds reside.

When bad things happen to us, at a conscious or unconscious level, we remember that event or that person or that situation with pain. "If we could only choose to forget the cruelest moments," says Lewis Smedes, "we could, as time goes on, free ourselves from their pain. But the wrong sticks like a nettle in our memory."[3] To rid ourselves of this nettle, we need what is sometimes called inner healing or healing of memories. This is a journey whose goal is to move from emotional imprisonment into full, abundant life.

Spiritual Wounds

Scripture says we are created in God's image and likeness. Spiritual wounds block us from living in that likeness. Types of wounds include:

1. *Wrong information about God.* "God gave you this disease" is the kind of false statement well-meaning people may make when we are experiencing the mystery of God and human suffering. What kind of a monstrous parent would want a disease for his or her child? And who would want to snuggle up to that kind of parent? Misinformation about God robs us of a healthy relationship with the one who loves us and wants to heal us.

2. *Lack of basic knowledge about God.* One woman began coming to church with her children after she heard her first-grade son say, "Who is 'God'?" when God was mentioned in a conversation. Despite religion's potential for harm, it does help us answer that question. It teaches us how to pray and how to see life in a wholesome way. Without that, on what foundation do we stand when a life-tremor registers 7.4 on our Richter scale?

3. *An addiction.* Poor choices can damage our God-given free will. An addiction to drugs, work, food, or whatever is a spiritual wound, a compulsion that overpowers our best intentions. Step-by-step, the addiction becomes an idol that replaces love and health and all that is good. One of Christianity's well-known saints, St. Augustine, was addicted to sex prior to his conversion. Sex was his god:

> I was held fast, not in fetters clamped upon me by another, but by my own will, which had the strength of iron chains....My will was perverse and lust had grown from it, and when I gave in to lust, habit was born, and when I did not resist the habit it became a necessity. These were the links which together formed what I have called my chain, and it held me fast....Two wills within me, one old, one new, one the servant of the flesh, the other of the spirit, were in conflict and between them they tore my soul apart.[4]

4. *Sin.* Sin is a misuse of God's gift of free will. Scripture assures us, however, that when we choose to sin, healing is available:

> I am writing this to you, my children, so that you will not sin; but if anyone does sin, we have someone who pleads with the Father on our behalf—Jesus Christ the righteous one. And Christ himself is the means by which our sins are forgiven, and not our sins only, but the sins of everyone. (1 John 2:1–2 GNT)

Praise God, John puts no limits on God's forgiveness as regards the seriousness or frequency of a sin. But as with any illness, sin must be acknowledged before it can be healed. We must "know the truth" (i.e., admit a failing to ourselves) before the Truth (Christ) can set us free.

Relational Wounds

Prisoners of war often report that their worst torture was solitary confinement. That's because from birth onward, relationships are essential to our very survival. And that is why relational wounds have such power to shatter lives and ripple out to others. Types of relational wounds include:

1. *A wounded relationship with a faith community.* Those who call themselves ex-Catholics or ex-fundamentalists or "ex" any other faith tradition can describe their pain in vivid detail. We open our souls to others every time we share our spirituality with them. Therefore any crushing of our spirituality also crushes our soul, our inner spirit.

2. *A wounded relationship with God.* Often this arises in the aftermath of a tragedy when, at a time we most need to hear God's voice, we seem to hear nothing. Or it may arise from unrealistic expectations of God, especially the expectation that if we are loving and holy, nothing bad will ever happen to us or our family. Jesus' experience on Good Friday should have dispelled this belief, but it persists. When bad things happen to good people, God often gets the blame.

3. *Wounded family relationships.* Years ago, neighbors tearfully told our family they were getting divorced. Despite outside help and heroic efforts, these good people had hurt each other. We could see pain in them and in their toddler as the latter's development regressed and temper tantrums appeared. But my husband and I also felt pain. If divorce could happen to this couple who loved God and prayed together, would our marriage be the next to crumble? Inexplicably, the collapse of someone else's marriage seemed to damage ours.

Perhaps relational wounds hurt so much because, like it or not, we all are one. Therefore, someone else's suffering becomes ours as well. When they hurt, we hurt; when they need healing, we need healing. Even with strangers, we are one and cannot escape that fact.

One Person, Indivisible

When I was growing up, my alarmist mother often warned me of the dangers of blisters. Her warning usually included a recitation of the story of Calvin Coolidge's teenage son, who developed a blister on a toe while playing tennis. Days later the blister killed him; he died of blood poisoning.

Just as this boy's toe injury destroyed his entire body, a wound in any dimension of our being damages our entire self. Each of us is an indivisible person, not a cluster of islands where the body lives on one island, the spirit on a second, the emotions on a third, and relationships on the fourth. And at any point in time, we probably have an array of wounds that need healing. Therein lies the challenge: When life is rocky and we recognize our need for healing, how do we know where to focus our attention? Do we start with the body, the mind, the spirit, or relationships? If we are indeed indivisible, where do we begin the healing journey?

No formula exists, just common sense. And common sense suggests starting with one symptom and seeing where it leads. For instance, Chris's most obvious symptom was high blood pressure. Therefore his journey toward health started with doctors and medication.

Eventually Chris began to look at causes of his problem. He knew one cause was genetic because three of his grandparents had died from strokes. But a spiritual wound may have contributed to his illness as well: Chris knew next-to-nothing about God; therefore when life got tough he had few places to turn for strength, wisdom, and assurance. And that pesky thing called mortality had begun to nibble at the edges of his consciousness. These issues were impacting his day-to-day responses to stress.

So in addition to medical care, Chris decided to enter into the Catholic Church's Rite of Christian Initiation of Adults (RCIA) program. Eighteen months later he was baptized, confirmed, and received first communion at the Easter Vigil, an experience he still describes as being like "coming home" and "starting life all over again." He experienced a peace he had never before known. This added to the positive effects of his blood pressure medication. In the end, more than Chris's body was healed. His soul was healed, too. The latter heightened the healing of the former.

That's what happens when we allow God into our pain: Our goal may be limited—cure of migraine headaches, for instance—and God wants that for us. But at the same time God also offers us a fullness of life that will surpass our dreams. As we open ourselves to healing and to God, results often exceed our expectations. When we need healing, God says this:

> ...I know the plans I have for you, says the Lord, plans for your welfare and not for harm, to give you a future with hope. Then when you call upon me and come and pray to me, I will hear you. When you search for me, you will find me; if you seek me with all your heart, I will let you find me, says the Lord, and I will restore your fortunes. (Jer 29:11–14a)

For You

As noted in the introduction, healing requires active participation. Therefore, each chapter in this book will include a section for your reflection. This first one focuses solely on pinpointing the need for healing. (Subsequent chapters will concentrate on healing options and activities.) The goal here is to help you assess where you are now and where you want to go. I invite you to reflect on as many of the following questions as you like. You may find it helpful to jot down answers on paper:

1. Where are you feeling the need for healing at this point in time? What are the various symptoms you are suffering from these days?

2. What kind of needs are these? Physical (e.g., cancer, bipolar disorder, an injury)? Emotional (e.g., grief, a childhood wound, posttraumatic stress)? Spiritual (e.g., sin, an addiction—your own addiction, not someone else's)? Relational (e.g., woundedness from a divorce; alienation from a friend, loved one, or faith community)?

3. Having looked at all these needs, ask yourself which one is bothering you the most right now. What need do you want to deal with the most? What is your most obvious symptom—the strongest need for healing you're aware of?

4. How long have you been dealing with this symptom/problem/need?

5. How has it affected other areas of your life?

6. If you are choosing to embark on a healing journey, and if you are comfortable with the idea of God communicating with you, I invite you to imagine the same question being addressed to you that Jesus asked the blind beggar named Bartimaeus. Imagine God asking you, "What do you want me to do for you?" (Mark 10:51). How would you answer that question? What do you want to say to God at this point in your healing journey?

In closing, I invite you to reflect on a scripture passage:

[T]his I call to mind,
  and therefore I have hope:
The steadfast love of the Lord never ceases,
  his mercies never come to an end;
they are new each morning;
  great is your faithfulness.
"The Lord is my portion," says my soul,
  "therefore I will hope in him." (Lam 3:21–24)

CHAPTER 2

The Ideal Healing

...I have set before you life and death....Choose life so that you and your descendants may live. (Deut 30:19)

One Sunday our Santa-shaped deacon gave a homily in which he talked about a near-perfect Saturday he'd recently had. After fighting the menace of a weedy lawn for several hours, he walked into his house, followed the scent of something delicious, and there in the kitchen discovered a fresh batch of heaven: double-chocolate brownies. "In a blink, two brownies were in a bowl," he said, "topped with a triple scoop of chocolate ice cream, chocolate syrup, and fresh raspberries." To complete this royal moment, he turned on a classical music station as he settled into an easy chair. Spoon poised, first succulent bite about to hit the taste buds, an ad interrupted his bliss: "The Heart Center at Providence would like to know: What healthy choices have you made for your heart today?"

Isn't that the way it is these days? A guy can't even sit down and savor his favorite dessert. Via every communication source known to humankind—ads, articles, doctors, friends, relatives, TV specials, and so on—the Health Patrol is out in full force. Eat less, exercise more, lose weight, go to bed early, floss your teeth, yackety yackety, nag nag nag. And pity today's smokers, whose addiction is about as politically correct now as leprosy was two thousand years ago.

The worst part about these unwanted messages is that they're right. If they weren't, we could wave them off like gnats at a picnic (a high-calorie, fat-laden picnic, by the way). But when we're honest with ourselves, we must admit they speak the truth. Often it's a truth we'd rather ignore because if we truly faced it, we might have to do something about it. We might have to change our lifestyle.

The Ideal Healing

The ideal healing is to be "healed" before we get sick. Nowhere is participation in our own healing clearer than in preventative medicine—"health maintenance" as it's sometimes called. This type of healing tends to reside at the bottom of most people's list of favorites, but the reality is, actions have consequences and God never takes away the natural consequences of those actions. If I jump off a cliff, my Savior will not suspend the law of gravity for my benefit. If I shun dentists, my teeth will rot. If I have sex with multiple partners, I'll catch venereal diseases. In short, if I make harmful choices, eventually I will need healing. My suffering won't be God's Will. Instead it will be the result of hurtful choices. The opposite, of course, is to make life-giving choices, but this requires a surprising amount of energy, awareness, and commitment. It also requires God's grace.

The Challenge to Choose Life

Every day each of us rolls out of bed and faces dozens of subtle choices for life or death. Do we exercise, or let our muscles shrivel? Do we spend time in prayer, or rush into the day? Do we mentally admit it when we're irritated, or deny our feelings? Over the years these tiny decisions add up to health or to sickness.

A popular ad used to show athletes clad in Nike shoes as they dashed and leapt around like Greek gods. "Just do it!" the ad urged. "Just do it" probably works for each of us in some areas of our lives. But I've never met anyone for whom willpower was enough in every area. Adam and Eve chose death in the Garden of Eden and we, their descendants, have inherited the character weakness that arose from their decision. Weakness tempts us to reject life in some aspect of our being: physical, emotional, spiritual, relational. When we succumb, by default we choose death in that part of our being. For instance, athletes may have no trouble talking themselves into maintaining physical fitness, but prayer? Climbing Mt. McKinley might be simpler. I, on the other hand, love prayer and avoid exercise.

The Power to Choose Life

The power to choose life includes at least four components: openness, motivation, good habits, and God's grace.

Openness

Our deacon loves to sink into prayer. Every day he chooses life in that part of his being. However, he also loves to sink into his easy chair with immense fudge sundaes. On the Saturday when God, via a radio ad, invited him to choose life for his heart, he looked at the dessert, looked at the radio, looked at the dessert...then turned off the radio. "You have to be open to hearing a message," he told our congregation. On that particular day, he wasn't open.

Motivation

The story is told of a large company whose board decided they wanted 100 percent participation in the firm's charity fund. Hold-outs would be called in for a chat with their boss, who would offer sterling reasons to be a donor. If that didn't work, the next higher ranking boss would talk with the employee.

One man was especially reluctant to contribute to the fund. So he kept having to meet with executives at a higher and higher level until finally he found himself in the office of the president. The president's message was succinct: Be a contributor or be fired. When the man told his coworkers he had decided to donate to the fund, they asked him why he had changed his mind. "It's simple," he replied. "No one before had explained the donor benefits to me quite so clearly."

That's motivation. We see the benefits of doing something and then choose to do it. Some stimulus—a conversation, an accident, an illness, a TV program, a scripture reading—spurs us to act at a time when we're open. Where previously we may have been reluctant or unaware, an incentive changes our mind. Now we have the energy and inspiration we need.

For example, in chapter 1 Chris's motivation to get his blood pressure checked came after a newspaper article and two conversations all took place during one week. Without those stimuli he might not have felt inspired to control his blood pressure until after a stroke. That would have been tragic, but often that's when motivation occurs—after an illness strikes, after a relationship collapses, after an addiction harms innocent people. This is sad and it isn't God's Will, but God always accepts us and loves us where we are and reaches out to offer us "a future full of hope." Every day the response is up to us. The choice is ours.

Good Habits

My husband and I used to begin each day with a good habit: He jogged and I prayed. I joked that together, we were quite fit. But of course as individuals, each of us lacked something. He lacked a relationship with God and I could have been an exhibit in a couch potato display. Health issues motivated us to add each other's habit to our daily schedule. Now he spends part of each lunch hour in prayer, and I exercise at 6:00 a.m.

Some experts say it takes thirteen weeks to develop a habit. Prior to then, a behavior change feels strange, as though it's not a part of who we are. So it's normal to initially struggle and expend extra energy to motivate ourselves to maintain our commitment. But after a few months have passed, the new behavior settles into our life pattern. The struggle eases. Now that we have developed a life-giving habit, it feels strange when we skip it.

Books about good habits we should develop occupy miles of shelf space. Eating, sleeping, exercising, relaxing, relating, praying, worshiping with others, getting regular check-ups: the list extends into near-infinity. As a friend once groused, "I've been told to do so many good things for my body, mind, and spirit each day that if I did them all, I'd have no time for anything else." Indeed. Yet God never asks the impossible of us.

Perhaps the best approach is a balanced one: some of each of the above habits. To achieve this, we need God's grace.

God's Grace

For me, one of the most startling statements in scripture is John 5:30: "By myself I can do nothing." Jesus said that. I've always believed that alone, he could not have raised Lazarus or walked on water or judged people. But in John 5, I hear that during Jesus' time on earth, he couldn't even put his feet out of bed in the morning without his Abba's grace. He needed grace every day for every action, every choice.

What was true for Jesus surely must be true for us: Regardless of whether we're in touch with our need for God's grace, we can do nothing without it. Alone, a rebellious or weak part of our being will periodically assert itself and grapple with another part of our being—the part that knows the best choice. Then we experience St. Paul's struggle: "I do not understand my own actions. For I do not do what I want, but I do the very thing I hate....Wretched man that I am! Who will rescue me from this body of death?" (Rom 7:15, 24). Paul's answer, and ours as well, comes in the next verse: "Thanks be to God through Jesus Christ our Lord!"

Grace combines with our God-given gift of free will. What happens then is an experience of power, the power to choose life in areas and ways we never before have had. This can be exhilarating. Better yet, it leads to healing. Best of all, it increases the likelihood we will attain the ideal: Get healed before we get sick.

For You

The "for you" section at the end of chapter 1 was designed to help you become aware of where you desire healing. What follows builds on that:

1. First, I invite you to place the details of your current life before God. Imagine that God is speaking to you personally when he says, "I set before you life and death. Choose life."

2. Now ask God to show you where you are choosing life in the area of physical health (e.g., good eating habits). Spend a few minutes thanking God for giving you the grace to make those choices.

3. After the time of thanksgiving, ask God to gently show you where you are falling short in behavior that affects your physical health (e.g., lack of daily exercise). Is there a reason for this? What options exist for changing this

pattern? Ask the Holy Spirit to show you reasons and options and to empower you to choose life in this area.

I suggest doing the above reflection for, say, fifteen minutes a day over a period of four days, each time looking at another area of your life: emotional, spiritual, and relational.

If you are like many, you may be tempted to focus only on your negative choices. But skipping the positive will leave you feeling bad about yourself and will also prevent you from seeing the graces God has given you. So don't overlook the positive. You already are choosing life in a number of ways. This prayer experience gives you a chance to thank God for that fact. It also offers you an opportunity to expand your healthy choices.

Looking Ahead

"Apart from me you can do nothing," Jesus told his followers (John 15:5). God's healing and the power to choose life come to us through a profusion of resources. The next chapter explores some of those resources.

CHAPTER 3

Using All of God's Gifts

Every good gift...comes down from God. (Jas 1:17 GNT)

When I was a child, a neighbor in the prime of life dis-covered he had lung cancer. Doctors told him he had six months to live. My father later told me that the man and his wife sat down and grappled with their options for avoiding this sudden death sentence. They lumped their choices into two categories—medical and religious—then selected one: medical. So he went to the Mayo Clinic instead of Lourdes, received radiation instead of prayer, and saw doctors instead of ministers. He only utilized the religious option the day before he died, when a priest gave him the last rites.

Back then, I didn't question the division of healing into medical versus religious, but now I think it's tragic and artifi-cial. It's like realizing we have two eyes and then agonizing over which eye to use, the right or the left.

James said, "every good gift comes down from God." If that's true, then it isn't only prayer and religious healing that come from God; good medicine does too; and so do self-help groups and support groups and psychology and preventative care. Why, then, don't we always make use of "all that is good" when we know we need healing? One reason may be non-awareness of the depth and breadth of God's gifts available to us for healing.

Resources for Healing

When my neighbor got sick in the 1950s, resources were scarce. Even the medical options for treating lung cancer were limited: surgery and radiation. And back then, the sacrament of anointing of the sick that Catholics received was called extreme unction and was not thought of as a healing sacrament. Instead, it was given moments before death.

Today, resources have burgeoned. God offers us many gifts to use for healing. Some of them lie within (e.g., private prayer). But many lie beyond our personal boundaries. These include:

1. *Traditional medical care.* This comes to us via doctors, nurses, physical therapists, and so on.

2. *Alternative medicine (e.g., herbal medicine, massage, acupuncture, biofeedback).* Once scorned by traditional medicine as fake, these now are being studied by the National Institutes of Health to see what works and what doesn't. Results used to be measured in anecdotes: "This did wonders for me. Why not try it?" Now, standard testing is helping everyone make informed choices.

3. *Counseling and psychotherapy.* These once were seen as something that only the insane or the desperate utilized. Today we know that mental health plays a huge role in overall health. Counseling/psychotherapy can help us achieve wellness in more than just our minds.

4. *Self-help groups.* Where would we be without groups like Alcoholics Anonymous? Addictions play havoc on people's health and lives. "Anonymous" groups have brought healing and hope to millions of addicts, their loved ones, and society as a whole.

5. *Support groups.* Research shows we do best when we don't feel alone in an illness. That's why support groups for

people with particular illnesses or problems improve the health and well-being of those who belong to them. As isolation decreases, hope and healing increase.

6. *Religious healing and pastoral care.* My neighbor thought his only religious option for healing was Lourdes. Today, he would have many choices, including prayer ministry, anointing of the sick, healing services, and books such as this one.

7. *Preventative medicine.* My neighbor smoked cigarettes back before the surgeon general announced they caused cancer. Now we know more about the innumerable factors that enhance or harm our health and longevity. Applying what we know is still hard, but at least we know.

Obstacles to Using God's Gifts

When I look at all of God's gifts, I see their richness. But I also see a number of obstacles to using them.

Insurance Woes

In 1995 a doctor recommended I get tested for a sleep disorder because regardless of how rested I was, I kept falling asleep while driving. So I phoned my insurance company for hospitalization preapproval. Their answer: "We won't tell you if we'll cover that test until after you take it." My response: "But that's an expensive test! If you won't cover it, then I won't schedule it." They remained adamant. I remained astonished.

Finally, I took the test without knowing if it was covered. Results showed I had an inherited condition called "central nervous system hypersomnia." Now a pill before a long drive keeps me awake and alert. America's highways and I are safer, thanks to God's gift of modern medicine but no thanks to my insurance company. They finally covered the cost of testing and medication, but not before a clerk tried to deny payment by calling it a psychiatric illness and saying they didn't cover that.

Stories like this reveal a huge challenge in today's world. I don't think insurance companies are the antichrist. Nevertheless, they can be a major barrier between us and God's healing gifts.

Lack of Knowledge of Where to Find the Best Outside Resources

A man once told me his wife had developed a rare form of glaucoma. Diagnosis required the skills of the best specialists in the nation; treatment was even trickier. Fortunately, the man telling me about his wife was, himself, an ophthalmologist. He knew the names and locations of all the top clinics and experts. And what he didn't already know, he easily discovered through contacts with his wider professional community.

Few of us are blessed with in-house specialists like this. Instead, when we need healing we must find help ourselves. If the need is physical, who is the best physician for the problem? Is alternative medicine a good option as well? What are the costs? The side effects? Similar questions apply if the need is emotional: Is medication the way to go? How about counseling too? How many sessions will insurance cover? Could a support group help? If so, where is an effective one?

Questions like these swirl through the mind no matter what the need. We become our own researcher. Like a good reporter, we ask who, what, where, when, why, and how questions. An excellent place to start is with current contacts (e.g., physicians, friends, faith community). But it's possible to extend the search via marvels such as the Internet. Then the problem becomes data overload. With all these choices, which are the best ones for this particular situation? The mind boggles.

Difficulty in Accessing and Using Resources

In separate accidents, two twelve year olds fell and suffered nearly identical head injuries. One of them recovered; one of them died. The difference was geography: One accident took place six blocks from a hospital while the other occurred up in the mountains.

What holds true for accessing resources for physical healing is true in other situations as well. For instance, with today's shortage of priests, many Catholics have lost access to pastoral care from ordained ministers. In some areas the ratio of laity to priests is 10,000:1. With those numbers, how many are able to experience spiritual healing through a parish priest?

Other barriers to accessing and using quality resources may be economic (e.g., lack of insurance). Whatever the cause, it's tragic that help is available for some but not for all. This means that some who could be healed will not be healed.

Reluctance to Use Outside Resources

The above obstacles to healing are external and may be outside our control. Another impediment lies within: We may be reluctant to use outside resources. Thoughts might be:

"That shot/test/treatment will hurt. I'm not going to do it."

"I once knew someone who died during surgery, so I'm never going to let anyone cut me open."

"It can't be that long since I last saw a dentist/doctor. I'm too busy right now. I'll schedule an appointment later."

"Nothing I've tried has worked. Why try something else? It wouldn't work either."

"If I ignore this, it will go away."

"Only wimps need help, and I'm not a wimp."

Healing often does involve pain, and who wants pain? Also, it takes courage, humility, and openness to turn to others and say, "Help!" At some level, we know if we place our trust in others, they might harm us. Trusting others is an act of faith in God and in the helpers. It's hard to make that act of faith.

The Power of Multiple Resources

Multiple resources bring us the healing power of each resource. Each is from God, and each contains unique gifts. Together these bring us more life and more healing than any single resource can do apart from the others.

For instance, a woman named Mary was diagnosed, like my childhood neighbor, with cancer that had spread. Unlike my neighbor, she turned to multiple resources for help. Medical care consisted of surgery, radiation, and chemotherapy. For psychological care, Mary went to a counselor who specialized in clients with cancer. Sessions eased her fear of dying, helped her deal with concerns about how family members were coping with her illness, and showed her ways to make some lifestyle changes. Also, Mary's physician referred her to a cancer-support group, where members encouraged one another in and through their shared journey.

For spiritual care, Mary received the sacrament of anointing of the sick, which she felt strengthened her and gave her courage. She also received weekly prayer ministry with a trained team. Ministry included prayers for maximum effectiveness of the medical treatments and minimum side effects. Ministry also helped her deal with issues such as where God was in her suffering. Best of all, Mary was able to experience God's healing presence at a deep level of her being.

It's been five years since Mary's medical treatments ended. She remains cancer-free and alive in ways she says she never was prior to her illness. Getting well was an all-out effort for a year, but it was a year that changed her life. She's grateful for

God's gift of life, and tells everyone that without all the help she received, she doesn't think she'd be here today.

Jesus says, "Seek and you will find" (Luke 11:9b), but that takes time and energy. I sometimes long for a magician with a wand rather than a savior who walks with me and empowers me to find and utilize many resources for healing. But God insists on saving each of us in ways that do more than take away our pain. The goal, as always, is transformation—new life that lasts.

For You

This section builds on the ones at the end of chapters 1 and 2, while chapters 13 and 14 will cover it in greater depth. Here, the goal is to begin looking at the breadth of resources available to you for healing.

1. Where have you found help in the past when you needed healing? What kind of resources were these—psychological? Medical? Spiritual? Which ones were helpful? Were any of them unhelpful?
2. Recalling where you currently are seeking more fullness of life, what resources are you using to obtain this? What kind of resources are these?
3. What kind of resources are you not now using for healing? If there are reasons for that—other than not having thought of it—what are those reasons (e.g., insurance woes, fear, lack of knowledge of where to find help)?
4. If you want to try a new resource for healing, I suggest praying for the gift of wisdom as to where to locate quality care. You may also feel the need to pray for courage to reach out and ask for help.

Looking Ahead

Medical and psychological resources for healing tend to be more widely known than spiritual ones. Therefore, part 2 (chapters 4 through 12) covers healing through prayer.

Two thousand years ago the disciples said, "Lord, teach us to pray" (Luke 11:1). And so he did. Today we're still learning about prayer and still being healed through it. That is the focus of what follows.

PART TWO

Healing through Prayer

CHAPTER 4

Prayer Power; Prayer Myths

Are any among you suffering? They should pray.
(Jas 5:13a)

The numbers are in and the word has gone forth: Prayer
works. Healing happens through prayer. Arthritis abates,
asthma lessens, depression improves, high blood pressure drops,
posttraumatic stress eases, addictions are given up, relationships are restored. These and more happen again and again
through the power of prayer.

What religious people have known for millennia, medical
and scientific communities now confirm through studies.
Physician and researcher Dr. Larry Dossey believes that if
prayer were a new drug or surgical technique, it would be proclaimed a scientific breakthrough.[1]

So why isn't there a mass movement toward daily prayer?
It's available everywhere at any time of the day or night—no
waiting rooms, no invasive procedures, no insurance forms, no
payments! Perhaps that's part of the problem: Can something
that costs nothing be worth anything?

Another problem is more subtle: Our culture believes many
myths about prayer, most of them unconscious and unstated.
Because unconscious beliefs have more power over us than if

we bring them to light and look at them, this chapter describes six popular prayer myths that harm our ability to pray and, through prayer, be healed.

Myth: "Prayer is for the holy—and I'm not holy."
Reality: Prayer is primarily relationship. Prayer is for everyone, the holy and the not-so-holy. God invites every person on earth to enter into relationship with him, but this is not a relationship of equals. Whenever we come before God, we come not as holy people; we always come as people in need of God's love, mercy, and healing.

If we tell ourselves we're not holy enough to pray, we miss the "fullness of life" Jesus offers us. But it's hard to move beyond this myth and recognize that prayer is as much for us as it was for the apostles.

Myth: "Prayer is a technique. If I study and learn the technique well, I'll be a good pray-er."
Reality: Prayer is a gift. No one has ever formed a professional league for people of prayer because without God's grace, the finite cannot communicate with the Infinite. We are totally dependent on God. "That we pray at all is a gift of God," wrote St. Augustine. It takes humility to acknowledge this much need and to ask the Holy Spirit to empower us with the gift of prayer.

Myth: "I decide to pray; I'm the one who initiates it."
Reality: Prayer is our response to God. Even a desire for prayer and healing is a response to God's desire to speak with us and heal us. We are like the woman at the well (John 4:1–41). What happens at that well is described in the Catholic Church's catechism:

The wonder of prayer is revealed beside the well where we come seeking water: there, Christ comes to meet every human being. It is he who first seeks us and asks us for a drink. Jesus thirsts; his asking arises from the depths of God's desire for us. Whether we realize it or not, prayer is the encounter of God's thirst with ours. God thirsts that we may thirst for him.[2]

Myth: "There's one type of prayer that's best for healing."
Reality: Prayer is an opening of the heart and mind to God. Healing through prayer happens not because we say the right words or claim the right scripture passage or use any other technique. It happens because whenever we open our heart and mind to God, something good happens; some sort of healing occurs. It may be a tiny, baby-step healing, it may take awhile for us to realize what has happened, and it may not be precisely what we have requested, but something good always happens whenever we reach out to God. We are changed.

Although there's no single type of prayer that's best, different prayer forms do appeal to different temperaments. (Prayer forms are described in the next several chapters.) The challenge is to find which prayers work best for us, which ones help us open our heart and mind to God.

Myth: "Prayer takes a lot of time. Some have time for it. I don't."
Reality: Prayer is a battle for everyone. If Christ is the bridegroom and each of us is the bride, then we are in a spiritual marriage where, ideally, we spend time with our beloved each day: one-on-one time during the week, and within our faith community on Sundays. The prayer aspect of the journey toward healing asks us to commit some of our time to the Lord each day. Making time for prayer is a battle, yet even five minutes focused solely on God can move us toward healing. Better

yet, it can provide the love we need to keep us well and healthy. It can enable us to deal with burdens that might otherwise make us sick in body, mind, and/or spirit.

Myth: "If I get distracted when I pray, or if my prayers feel 'blah,' I haven't prayed well."

Reality: Prayer is a mystery. St. Paul freely admitted his struggles when he told the Romans: "We do not know how to pray as we ought" (Rom 8:26). Nevertheless, God invites us to enter into prayer and even grapple with it when necessary. No matter how skilled we become, an element of mystery will always remain because we are creatures in relationship with our Creator. We will never "arrive" at excellence.

It's tempting to approach prayer not as part of a relationship but as a performance, like being a figure skater at the Olympics. We're the skater and God is the judge who holds up a card at the end of our routine—5.9 on a day when we stay focused on God and feel all sorts of blessings. On a day when thoughts collide with prayer like a skater falling to the ice, we can imagine the divine judge frowning and holding up a 2.1 card. In reality, it is we who hold up both the "good" and "bad" cards. God always is pleased with prayer. What counts is our intention to pray, our desire to pray, our decision to pray. Performance may matter to us, but not to God. Even a pitiful attempt at prayer is, in fact, prayer.

Conclusion

Add up the myths that lie buried beneath the radar signals of the human mind, and should it surprise us that prayer often is turned to as a last resort for healing? To move beyond myths and the idea that prayer is a when-all-else-fails tool, I invite you to reflect on the following.

For You

Reflect on your personal experience of the six prayer truths described in this chapter:

1. *A relationship with God.* Have you ever been aware of God's presence with you? Or is this something that seems to happen only to others, not to you? If you've ever had a one-on-one experience of God, what was it like?
2. *A gift from God.* Do you ever feel incapable of praying? If you have ever asked God for the gift of prayer, was it easier for you to pray afterward?
3. *Your response to God.* Have you ever experienced God reaching out to you, especially when you were in need? If so, what was that like? Were you able to respond? Did you recognize that as prayer?
4. *An opening of your heart and mind to God.* Have you ever experienced something good happening to you as a result of opening your heart and mind to God? Has it ever resulted in some sort of emotional, physical, or spiritual healing?
5. *A battle.* If prayer is a battle for you, what is your greatest struggle? For example, time shortage? Boredom? Anger, fear, or disillusionment with God?
6. *A mystery.* It's difficult to live with mystery, to accept the fact that prayer is something we can practice but never completely master. How much, or how little, does this bother you?

Looking Ahead

Some people structure prayer around the acronym ACTS: adoration, contrition, thanksgiving, supplication. This can bring more healing and more fulfillment than the common tendency to focus solely on asking God for things (i.e., focusing only on supplication). The next three chapters cover these prayer ingredients: praise (a blend of adoration and thanksgiving), contrition, and supplication.

In addition to prayer ingredients, rich prayer forms have been used and taught for centuries. Hurting people have experienced God's healing touch through scripture meditation, spiritual journaling, contemplation, and a host of other types of prayer. Chapters 8 through 11 look at some prayer forms through which healing can occur. Finally, chapter 12 explores ways to find the prayers that work best for you, plus how to fit prayer into a busy life.

"Find out for yourself how good the Lord is" (Ps 34:8 GNT). Find out for yourself how prayer can lead to healing.

CHAPTER 5

Prayer of Praise

Rejoice always, pray without ceasing, give thanks in all circumstances; for this is the will of God in Christ Jesus for you. (1 Thess 5:16–18)

Years ago, police in an oppressive regime seized two men, dragged them off, and beat them. Their crime? Being Christian and talking to others about their faith. Bleeding and bruised, the men were finally thrown into a jail cell and shackled to a wall. By that night, they had decided how to respond to their pain: They began to pray and sing praises to God.

This was no evil event from the days of Communism. This was Paul and Silas's experience. Acts 16:26 recounts what happened next: "Suddenly there was an earthquake, so violent that the foundations of the prison were shaken; and immediately all the doors were opened and everyone's chains were unfastened." The jailer ended up taking Paul and Silas to his home, washing their wounds, and begging them to baptize him and his family.

How many could praise God in the midst of such pain and filth? More appropriate responses would be anger, weeping, or plotting an escape. Prayers of praise in that setting seem out of place or even crazy.

Baffled feelings like these arose the first time I attended a prayer meeting. People were going on and on praising God.

Eventually, I learned why. I learned what praise is and what its benefits are.[1]

What Praise Is

Praise is a joyful response to any positive event in our lives. At concerts, we applaud. When our team scores, we cheer. But bleeding in prison? How could that be a positive event? And when we're in need, who but a masochist could see it as a plus? Why praise God?

We do so in faith and in trust, believing what Paul told the Romans: "We know that all things work together for good for those who love God" (Rom 8:28). Moving into this faith and trust is a three-step process:

1. We recognize God's kindness to us.
2. Recognition gives rise to attitudes of awe, reverence, and gratitude.
3. Finally, we express our attitude in some external way. This may be vocal (e.g., singing or praying aloud). Or it may be through body language (e.g., raising our hands, kneeling). These convey our response to God's goodness to us. People call them by various names: praise, thanksgiving, blessing.

Implicitly or explicitly, praise also includes a desire for God's goodness to continue in the future, as Paul and Silas may have been doing. So the prayer includes phrases such as those spoken by the blind Bartimaeus as he sought healing: "Jesus, Son of David, have mercy on me!" (Mark 10:47). Bartimaeus could not have addressed Jesus with these words without first recognizing him as the loving, merciful, powerful Messiah.

Sources of Praise Prayers

1. *Scripture.* The Psalms overflow with thanksgiving for God's blessings. Also, the Bible contains many titles for God that are themselves a form of praise (e.g., Light of the world, Son of God).

2. *Liturgy.* The Mass includes a number of praise prayers, such as the Sanctus (Holy, holy, holy, Lord God of Hosts) and the Gloria.

3. *Litanies.* Litanies sound like petitions (e.g., "Jesus, our refuge, have mercy on us"). Actually, each statement contains an implied "you do." "Jesus, our refuge, [you do] have mercy on us."

4. *Hymns.* Music can touch people's spirits when nothing else reaches them. Hymnals overflow with songs of praise. Tapes and CDs help us pray these songs while driving, cooking, exercising, and so on.

5. *Tongues.* When the brain's supply of praise prayers runs low, the charismatic gift called "tongues" can move us beyond the limits of our own words.[2]

Benefits of Praise

1. *Praise opens the door to healing because it opens the door to God.* Saying or singing prayers of praise at the start of a prayer time can help us experience God's presence quickly. We may start out feeling low, but within minutes, praise prayers can help us be more hopeful or even joyful. This, in turn, opens us to healing.

2. *Praise makes us Christ-centered rather than need- or self-centered.* Illness and pain can turn our eyes inward until that's all we're able to see. Praise prayers help bring us out of that inner trap. As we look at God instead of ourselves, we discover God's love and power in our lives. When life wears a shroud of

gloom, a litany of praise can enable us to see beyond the darkness of our circumstances. The length of the litany may need to match the depth of our discouragement.

3. *In praise, God reveals himself to us.* Jesus tells us, "I am with you always, to the end of the age" (Matt 28:20b), but unless we experience that truth at a felt level, he might as well be in a different solar system. Praise prayers can help.

4. *Praise can heal relationships because it allows God into our pain.* For instance, one woman despaired about her teenagers because all she saw were their faults. One day she decided to start praising God for her children. Gradually she began seeing their positive traits, even those in the rough. Her feelings changed to ones of gratitude toward God and a growing love for her children. Praising God changed her focus and, ultimately, her heart.

5. *Praise frees us from slavery to our surroundings.* For me, praise's best benefit is its power to move me into joy. It enables me to be joyful, regardless of circumstances, and opens me to God's blessings. That's what happened to Paul and Silas: Praise prayers gave them mental freedom before an earthquake gave them physical freedom.

For You

We cannot muscle our way into praise any more than we can fly under our own power because "no one can say 'Jesus is Lord' except by the Holy Spirit" (1 Cor 12:3). Therefore, to pray the prayer of praise and experience its benefits, begin by asking God for the gift of praise.

Next, you may want to focus on an external praise stimulus. At church, this could mean joining in singing the hymns. At home, it could mean putting on a CD and singing to it, or reciting a litany or reading a praise psalm aloud. Your goal is for these outer words to move inward to become an act of faith and a response to God's goodness. An outside stimulus is a good place to start.

While focusing on that, start consciously bringing to mind an act of God you are grateful for. It may be something that affects your salvation (e.g., the birth of Jesus). Or it may be small (e.g., recovery from a cold). God's act may be big or little, cosmic or private.

Now allow an emotional response to God's act to rise up within you (e.g., gratitude, awe, love).

Finally, give this response some external expression—singing, praying out loud, and so on. The format is less important than the heart because praise is a prayer of the heart.

Conclusion

A few minutes spent in prayers of praise makes a wonderful start to any time of worship, whether a Sunday liturgy or a personal prayer time. It enhances all that follows and can open us to God's healing power. And beyond our times of prayer, praise helps us live out Peter's words:

> You are a chosen race, a royal priesthood, a holy nation, God's own people, in order that you may proclaim the mighty acts of him who called you out of darkness into his marvelous light. (1 Pet 2:9)

CHAPTER 6

Prayer of Contrition

The time is fulfilled, and the kingdom of God has come near; repent, and believe in the good news. (Mark 1:15)

Our first parents, Adam and Eve, were told they could "be like gods." They fell for the lie and disobeyed God. I've always wondered what would have happened to them and to us if they had accepted responsibility for their actions. When confronted by God, what if each had said, "Lord, I am sorry; I have sinned; have mercy on me; please forgive me"? Instead, Adam said, "The woman whom you gave to be with me, she gave me fruit from the tree, and I ate." And Eve said, "The serpent tricked me, and I ate" (Gen 3:12–13). In other words, the act could not be denied, but blame belonged elsewhere—on God, another person, or the devil.

Synonyms for contrition include regret, remorse, and repentance. We have wrestled with these from the dawn of humanity, and in the morning of Christianity's third millennium, the wrestling match continues. In fact,

> To mention the word sin today is to be laughed at. One must feel guilty about feeling guilty. And John the Baptist must feel like an idiot, for he went out into the desert "proclaiming a baptism of repentance that led to the forgiveness of sins" (Mark 1:4). He would be unemployed today."[1]

When we come before God in prayer, we come not as the gods Adam and Eve aspired to be. We come as creatures before the Creator, much-loved but fallible children before our all-loving Parent. When we have sinned, we bring that to God and humbly ask him to remove the sin and replace it with his grace.

The Challenges

Contrition is challenging in at least three ways:

1. Bringing a weakness before God can make us feel utterly exposed, as if we've lost even our skin.
2. It's easy to merge sin with condemnation. We're told to "hate the sin but love the sinner," a tough thing to do with others but even tougher to do with oneself.
3. It's easy to believe that God's love is as finite and conditional as human love and that he laments our very being, not just our behavior. Admitting an imperfection to ourselves and to God may give rise to feelings of humiliation, echoes of the world's unspoken message that we aren't really beloved children of God; deep down, we're loathsome.

That's not true, even at those times when Paul's words could be our own: "I do not understand what I do. [I am] a prisoner to the law of sin which is at work in my body" (Rom 7:15, 23 GNT). To deny a failing is to stay imprisoned, unhappy, and unhealed. The price of freedom is honesty.

I recall one of those moments of honesty in my life. I had inherited some heirlooms that I dearly loved—too dearly, I learned after I lost a cameo that had belonged to my grandmother. I felt as devastated as if I had lost a person, not a brooch. My husband and I dug through our car, retraced that evening's steps, prayed, and placed notices in newspapers.

No cameo. We eventually concluded that in all probability, someone with a finders-keepers-losers-weepers attitude had found it.

Finally, I turned to God in grief, expecting a celestial "there, there" pat on the head. Opening my Bible in search of comfort, I found myself staring at Luke 16:13 (GNT): "No servant can be the slave of two masters; [he] will hate one and love the other....You cannot serve both God and money." Well, I thought, Jesus can't be talking to me. I'll just look for another verse. The next one I turned to was Matthew 6:19–21 (GNT): "Do not store up riches for yourselves here on earth, where moths and rust destroy, and robbers break in and steal. Instead, store up riches for yourselves in heaven....For your heart will always be where your riches are."

Even if I had been unconscious, I couldn't have missed the fact that the finger of God was resting on my forehead, not in condemnation but in truth. And I sensed a message: Repent; say you're sorry; ask for the grace to focus on spiritual riches rather than earthly heirlooms.

So I repented, said I was sorry, and mentally released all my possessions to God. I also prayed that whoever had found the cameo would enjoy it and be blessed by its beauty. A sense of freedom began to wash over me as I realized my heirlooms had owned me, not I them. Walking outside after this prayer time, a burst of color struck my vision: May flowers in full bloom throughout our neighborhood. Their exceptional vividness brought to mind a musician's description of a near-death experience, where she had felt herself to be standing at the threshold of heaven: "No music," she told me. "Instead, I saw the most glorious, spectacular colors. I've never seen anything like it before or since."

That's what contrition/repentance can feel like—a gift of freedom that's so vibrant, it's like being at heaven's door. It fits my favorite definition of repentance: To repent is to change the direction in which we are seeking happiness. We turn away from sin; we turn to God.

For You

Ever since the time of Adam and Eve, avoidance has been contrition's biggest roadblock. Initially this prayer ingredient feels uncomfortable. Ignoring it is easy, but then the potential for healing through contrition is lost. To move beyond avoidance, steel your nerves, "gird your loins," ask God for the gift of courage, then try the following.

First, recall some event or attitude in your life that you regret. (Defer any possible "biggies" for the moment.) Next, bring the event/attitude and your feelings about it before God. Imagine God being as loving and welcoming as the father of the prodigal son (Luke 15:11–32). Express your regret in some way; tell God you're sorry.

Now imagine your compassionate Savior extending forgiveness to you in some way. If you feel condemnation instead of love and forgiveness, realize the condemnation doesn't come from God. Instead, it may be mental "tapes" from society or the past; or it may be the natural tendency to inflate expectations of oneself. Try to see beyond these; focus on God. What do you feel/think/mentally see? God wants to give you freedom and healing.

If the event or attitude you regret has involved another person (e.g., gossip or an argument) consider what possible actions you could take to remedy that situation. This can be hard to even think about. However, it fits with what Jesus asks us to do (Matt 5:24: "…first be reconciled to your brother or sister, and then come and offer your gift [to God]". Also, amazing healings happen to us and to others through the process of reconciliation.

Finally, take a few moments to thank God and enjoy your closeness to him, closeness that may have increased through this process of contrition.

CHAPTER 7

Prayer of Supplication

Ask and you will receive... (John 16:24)

A collection of third graders' thoughts about God included this: "One of God's main jobs is listening to prayers. There must be a terrible lot of noise in his ears. God sees everything and hears everything and is everywhere, which keeps him pretty busy. So you shouldn't go wasting his time by asking him for something your parents said you couldn't have."

"Asking God for something" is a good definition of supplication, which might best be summarized in one word: HELP! Sometimes we ask for help on our own behalf, in which case it's called a prayer of petition: "God help me." At other times we appeal on behalf of others, in which case it's called a prayer of intercession: "God help them." These requests arise from an awareness of our need for God.

Whether we're praying for ourselves or for others, we tend to do so in one of two ways: Specific prayers focus on a desired result (e.g., "God, heal my knee without surgery"). Open-ended prayers simply place a need in God's hands (e.g., "Thy will be done," "Lord, I want what you want," or a general "Lord, heal me"). Whichever we choose, our prayers are meant to flow naturally from our relationship with God: Bridegroom/spouse, Parent/child, Creator/creature. These are profound relationships of love and trust, not distance and doubt. So we can bring our requests to God in a spirit of trust.

What does this trust feel like or look like? Primarily, release. We bring a need to God and release it into his loving care. This can be done visually by, for instance, mentally placing a need at the foot of the cross. Or it can be expressed physically or in words. No matter how it's expressed, God invites us to pray in trust, and the essence of that trust is release. When we trust God, we are able to place our needs into his hands, believing he will do the most loving thing possible with them.

As noted in chapter 4, scientists can demonstrate that healing happens through prayers of supplication. Here are a couple of details from medical studies:[1]

1. The quantity of prayer influences the outcome. Praying only once for a particular healing is not as effective as praying for that healing once a day for, say, a month.
2. All prayer is effective, but researchers have discovered that open-ended requests are more likely to bring outcomes that are in the best interest of the sufferer. Because we do not know what's best for us and our loved ones, abandoning ourselves into God's care often works better than telling God what should happen, how it should happen, and when it should happen. God's dreams for us always surpass our dreams for ourselves.

Challenges

Jesus invites us to pray for help: "Ask and you will receive...," so we ask. But in the act of asking, four potential problems emerge.

Challenge #1: Treating a Prayer
of Supplication Like a Catalog Order

Here, we place a prayer order, pay for it, and await its arrival. If it fails to materialize within our expected time frame, we presume someone is at fault. Perhaps we failed to place the order correctly, or the company's computer is down, or mail service is sloppy. A catalog-order mind-set asks why the order hasn't arrived, then attempts to take corrective action.

No one consciously sees prayers of supplication as being like that, but when we ask God for something and hear nothing back except the sound of silence, our mind naturally tries to make sense out of what went wrong. Some common conclusions:

> "God is not loving. I'm not going to have anything more to do with him." (Translation: It's God's fault.)

> "I must not have enough faith" or "I didn't pray the right way; my prayers actually made things worse." (Translation: It's my fault.)

> "There's a lot of spiritual opposition these days. I'll have to bind and cast out the Enemy." (It's Satan's fault.)

> "Prayer doesn't work." (It's the fault of prayer itself.)

Thoughts like these say a lot about our image of God (e.g., cold, absent, erratic, weaker than Satan). They also say a lot about our image of ourselves (e.g., abandoned by God, powerful enough to order God around or create bad results) and about Satan (e.g., as strong as God). And our reasoning shows us our expectations of what will happen when we reach out to God with a need.

Challenge #2: "My Will Be Done, Lord, Not Yours"

This can take a variety of forms. Two common ones:

1. Saying a prayer so many times each day for so many days, or praying to particular saint.
2. "Claiming the promise" of a Bible passage. This arises from a belief that says God must live up to promises in scripture because the Lord cannot be untrue to himself. All that's needed is to find the right passage, "claim" it as true in our situation, then have faith that God will come through in the manner and time frame we desire.

Whatever the form, the unstated goal is to manipulate the Creator of the universe into doing what we want. A request made with the right words or the right scripture verses or the right number of times to the right saint will bring guaranteed results. And the message is that God is absent until aroused by fervent prayer; if a prayer isn't answered within the designated time frame, it's our fault. We didn't have enough faith, or we didn't pray the requisite number of times, or whatever.

When in extreme distress, who has not unwittingly attempted to manage God through prayers that promise to resolve that distress? We're frantic. How can we get our needs met? And if our needs aren't met, who is to blame? These are the unconscious questions that naturally swirl through the human mind when healing doesn't seem to be happening.

Challenge #3: Blindness to Results That Differ from the Hoped-For Outcome

It's common to pray for one type of healing and experience a different one instead. We're interested in one outcome—perhaps physical healing—but God cares about our entire being, emotional and spiritual as well as physical. The healing we seek often comes later rather than at once, but because we've received other types of healing along the way, we end up being better off than if our initial request had yielded instant results.

Speaking for myself, I can get irritated with God's delayed responses. Yes, I know that in the long run it's better to be healed at all levels of my being, but sometimes I say, "God, how about just a physical healing this time? Skip the deeper stuff. Right now I'm only interested in my lower back."

The challenge, then, is to be open to seeing and receiving results beyond what we have requested.

Challenge #4: Lack of Balance

Supplication used to occupy 99.99 percent of my prayer times because I didn't know other types of prayer existed. Once I started using other prayer forms, I felt liberated from the confines of the earlier "me" focus. And I began to see God as far more than Supreme Valet, filler of my needs.

Conclusion

God does want us to ask for blessings and for help. In doing so, however, we must remind ourselves that we aren't the Lord. We aren't even the lord of our own healing. The good news, however, is that when we approach God with our needs, we can trust the One who loves us. We can release our fears and pain into God's hands.

For You

What follows is one way to pray a prayer of supplication.

Begin by bringing to mind a need, preferably a small one rather than a huge one because it's more difficult to release major needs. Next, pray a prayer of praise or thanksgiving to help you experience God's presence with you in this prayer time.

Now spend a few minutes expressing your request in some way, focusing on releasing yourself and your need to God. It's easier to avoid a "catalog order" mentality if you stay away from telling God what to do and how to do it. By being as nondirected as possible, you open yourself to results in areas that may surprise and delight you.

Finally, end with a prayer of thanksgiving, then a reflection on how you feel: If you felt worried about the need before you prayed, do you feel less worried now? It takes time for trust to grow, so it may take a while to feel more peaceful about a need. When worry overwhelms us, sometimes the best we can do is release a concern to God for a nanosecond during prayer and not at all outside of prayer.

Also, even if you feel a sense of release during a prayer time, it's common for a concern to quickly resurface beyond that time. Keep on keeping on. Release the need to God again and again and again and again until you're so tired of it that you really are able to let it go.

Looking Ahead

Despite its capacity to open us to healing, prayer can bore us silly and diminish our motivation to make time for it. The next several chapters offer ways around that problem: some time-honored prayer forms, ideas for using them in healing, and ways to fit prayer into your daily life.

CHAPTER 8

Scripture Meditation

"Let the Word of Christ dwell in you richly." (Col 3:16)

In *Healing Ministry: A Practical Guide,* Father Leo Thomas described the emotional healing he received in 1948 when, in the aftermath of World War II, he was struggling with a severe case of post–traumatic stress disorder.

> At a pre-seminary retreat in the midst of that struggle, the retreat master asked everyone to meditate on Mark 10:46–52—Jesus' healing of the blind beggar. As I entered into the passage, its words seemed to be addressed just to me. Like Bartimaeus, I could feel myself calling, "Jesus! Son of David! Have mercy on me!" Then I sensed Jesus asking me, "What do you want me to do for you?" My answer was the same as Bartimaeus': "Teacher, I want to see again." The passage comforted me and helped me discern that God was calling me to become a priest. Its effect on me has persisted throughout my adult life."[1]

This example illustrates the healing power of scripture meditation, healing that occurs as we "let the Word of Christ, in all its richness, find a home" within our mind and soul. Different styles of this prayer form have arisen over the centuries, two of which are Ignatian and Augustinian.[2]

Ignatian-Style of Meditation

The Israelites of Hebrew Scriptures remembered and immersed themselves in their history in order to relive it. St. Ignatius of Loyola, founder of the Jesuits, developed that style of prayer and made it a key ingredient in his *Spiritual Exercises*.

In an Ignatian-style of meditation, we mentally enter into a Biblical scene and imagine ourselves as part of it. We can be anyone in the scene we choose to be: a sick person, a bystander, Jesus himself, someone who's giving Jesus a hard time—anyone. For instance, in the above example Father Thomas immersed himself in a first-century scene. He placed himself in Jesus' presence, with himself as Bartimaeus crying out "Jesus! Son of David! Have mercy on me!" He sensed Jesus asking, "What do you want me to do for you?" Within the meditation, he experienced being touched and healed.

Augustinian-Style of Meditation

St. Augustine of Hippo spent his early life being anything but saintly. A poster boy for self-indulgence, he lived for pleasure. Yet even in the midst of an addiction to debauchery, he heard God's call to holiness. His answer? Later. "Give me chastity and continence," he prayed, "but not yet." God kept up the pursuit until Augustine's inner turmoil became unbearable and reduced him to tears. Finally, as he wept in a garden one afternoon he heard a child in a nearby house singing the same words over and over: "Take it and read, take it and read."

> I stemmed my flood of tears and…hurried back to the place where I had put down the book containing Paul's Epistles. I seized it and opened it, and in silence I read the first passage on which my eyes fell: "Not in revel-

ing and drunkenness, not in lust and wantonness, not in quarrels and rivalries. Rather, arm yourselves with the Lord Jesus Christ; spend no more thought on nature and nature's appetite"....In an instant, as I came to the end of the sentence, it was as though the light of confidence flooded into my heart and all the darkness of doubt was dispelled."[3]

In the Augustinian-style of meditation, we hear God speaking to us in our present situation. Rather than going back in time, scripture events and words come forward to touch our lives in the here-and-now. A word spoken to Israelites or disciples or an individual in the Bible becomes a word bearing our own name. For instance, Isaiah 43:1 says, "Now thus says the LORD, he who created you, O Jacob, he who formed you, O Israel: Do not fear, for I have redeemed you; I have called you by name, you are mine." Here we would substitute our own name for Jacob/Israel. In the same way Augustine heard God saying "arm yourself with the Lord Jesus Christ," we would sense God saying: "Do not be afraid. I have saved you."

The Experience of Meditation

Scriptural experiences of God depend on how we tend to perceive reality. When using our God-given imagination, some of us mentally "see" something, as on a TV screen. Others mentally "hear" something. Still others feel something. In the Bartimaeus scene, Father Thomas heard Jesus asking, "What do you want me to do for you?" A visually oriented person might see himself or herself in the scene. Someone else might feel it without pictures or words. All these experiences are equally valid. All can be equally healing.

Mental pictures are not apparitions, such as the reported appearances of Mary at Lourdes. Instead, they are like an inner picture we see with our mind's eye. Inner voices are not actual voices but rather are thoughts inspired by the Holy Spirit. They feel natural and sound like our own voice but seem to come from beyond ourselves. Words from the Bible feel as though they are directed just to us. We open ourselves to God by giving him silent space and time. God, in turn, communicates to us personally, one-on-one, in the way we are best able to experience his healing presence.

Benefits of Scripture Meditation

In scripture meditation, the Holy Spirit inspires understanding and communicates to us as we focus on the Word of God—sometimes literally only a word or two. A meditation on Bartimaeus might never get beyond its opening phrase: "They came to Jericho...." Ten minutes of imagining ourselves walking next to Jesus, feeling his presence, can be incredibly healing as we experience for ourselves that "Jesus Christ is the same yesterday and today and forever" (Heb 13:8). We are not alone. The Risen Lord is with us, eager to heal.

Another benefit to scripture meditation is that this prayer form helps us see a healing need from God's perspective, not just our own. This, in turn, can help us discern what to do, or not do, about the need.

For You

Scripture meditation requires a quiet place, a Bible, and some uninterrupted time—fifteen minutes minimum, ideally thirty minutes to avoid feeling rushed.

Begin by selecting a scripture passage. (See ideas, below.) If you want to try an Ignatian-style of meditation, action-oriented Gospel passages often work well. I recommend a healing account, such as Mark 6:46–52.

Say a short opening prayer so as to focus on God, then ask for the gift of being able to meditate on the passage you've chosen.

Read through your passage once before meditating on it. Then read through it again very slowly, one phrase or sentence at a time. Pause whenever a word or sentence seems important. Imagine yourself in that scene, or imagine the words you've read being spoken to you in the present. Spend time soaking up the experience. Give your creative imagination permission to wander. Allow feelings to surface if they're inclined to do so. Set aside specific goals, even the goal of getting through a passage. Focus, instead, on experiencing yourself relating to God. This is one of the ways to receive healing. In the words of one woman, "You start your prayer one type of person; you end it another type of person." It usually takes months to recognize this.

End your meditation with a short prayer, perhaps of thanksgiving. To enrich your experience and heighten its healing power, consider the prayer form described in the next chapter: spiritual journaling.

Scripture passage ideas:

Ignatian:

> Matthew 14:22–33 (Jesus walks on water)
> Matthew 15:21–28 (Canaanite woman seeks healing for her daughter)
> Mark 14:32–42 (Agony in the Garden)
> Mark 10:46–52 (Jesus heals the blind Bartimaeus)

Augustinian (suggestion: change name[s] to your own name):

> Isaiah 43:1–5 ("Fear not...")
> James 5:14–15 ("Is there anyone who is sick?...")
> Romans 8:26–28 ("The Spirit comes to help us in our weakness...")
> John 8:1–11 (The woman caught in adultery)

CHAPTER 9

Spiritual Journaling

…Write the vision; make it plain on tablets. (Hab 2:2)

Kelly's head started hurting each day on her way to work. The mere thought of facing eight hours in the same building as her boss made every muscle tighten up. An experienced teacher with a record of success in the classroom, Kelly had accepted a job offer at a different school because she sought new challenges. What she found instead was a nightmare.

The principal turned out to be critical, mean-spirited, and brutally cold-hearted. She never passed up an opportunity to reprimand Kelly, while refusing to give any specifics as to how she might improve her job performance. When Kelly asked for suggestions, what she received instead was, "I shouldn't have to tell you. You should be professional enough to know what you're supposed to do."

Feeling devastated and battered, Kelly sought professional counseling. There she found support and a place to vent her anger and pain. Another place where she could express herself was on paper. During and after that year-from-hell, Kelly experienced the healing power of spiritual journaling.

Cardinal John Henry Newman described his experience of spiritual journaling as "praying through the tip of a pen." This prayer form gives voice to our journey with God, with our deeper self, and with others. It differs from keeping a diary, which primarily focuses outward to record events, travels, experiences, and, perhaps, our responses to them.

Expressing thoughts and feelings to God in writing can open our heart and mind to healing when we know we need it, as in Kelly's situation, and also when we have no idea of our need. It can take a variety of forms:

1. A response to a scripture meditation. Here, we write down part or all of a scripture verse we've been meditating on, then record our response to it. Some like to end the journal entry with a brief, written prayer.

2. A poem, song, drawing, or any other form of self-expression.

3. A letter to God. St. Augustine used this format in *Confessions:*

> I have learned to love you late, Beauty at once so ancient and so new! You were within me, and I was in the world outside myself. I searched for you outside myself....You were with me, but I was not with you.[1]

4. Personal thoughts and feelings, not addressed to anyone in particular and not in response to any outside question or scripture passage.

5. A written response to a reflection question put forth in a book or by a speaker. For example, many books by Matthew, Dennis, and Sheila Linn have reflection questions intended for use in healing. During Kelly's journey toward healing, she wrote responses to a number of questions from the Linns's *Don't Forgive Too Soon.*[2]

6. A letter to a person—not one that gets mailed, but one that's helpful in the healing process. For instance, *Don't Forgive Too Soon* suggests writing "the ideal letter of apology that you would want to receive from the person who hurt you."[3] Kelly

chose to do this after she had moved on to a new, rewarding teaching job. The letter turned out to be a key factor in her healing, in part because it helped her see that much of the abuse she had received arose not from her own failings but rather from her boss's woundedness. An excerpt from that letter:

Dear Kelly,

I'm sorry for all the pain I caused you in your year here. I have a tendency to see things in black and white. I therefore failed to see your imaginativeness and creativity.

I'm sorry I did not acknowledge your gifts as a teacher. You possess so much zeal for life—a spark which died in me long ago. My professional years are just ending, and I envy your beginning.

Most of all, I'm sorry for my part in your leaving here with such bad memories. I temporarily stamped out some of the joy in your soul. Know that you are loved by your students and their parents. And if anyone asks of you in the future, I will say I am proud to have known you.

Sincerely,
[Principal]

Benefits of Spiritual Journaling

Healing benefits of this prayer form include the following:

1. It helps us develop and express our relationship with God.

2. It helps us discover unknown parts of our inner self. ("I didn't know I felt like this" is a common thought during spiritual journaling.) The feelings might cover the whole range of human emotions (e.g., anger, bitterness, jealousy, deeper love than we realized, compassion).

3. Medical findings show that journaling promotes physical healing. In one study, patients with rheumatoid arthritis or asthma wrote about a traumatic event for just twenty minutes a day, three days in a row. Over half of them experienced marked, long-term improvement in their health. Why? Researches think it restored hormone balances.[4]

4. Expressing ourselves on paper liberates us from thoughts going around inside the head in endless, useless cycles. Voicing these thoughts/feelings/ideas on paper removes them from the mental racetrack of the mind. Putting them outside ourselves helps us gain perspective—often, God's perspective.

5. Finally, spiritual journaling allows us to look back on our journey with God to see where we've been, reexperience earlier blessings all over again, and move into deeper healing than when we made the original entry. Marvelous surprises await us when we accept God's invitation to "write the vision," or the thoughts or the words (Hab 2:2).

For You

There are no actual "how-tos" for journaling; it's meant to be totally free self-expression. You can do what you want, how you want, when you want, and where you want. What follows, then, are simply a few ideas for how to free yourself to engage in this form of prayer.

First, of course, you need materials to write (or draw) with. Some use computers; others feel freer with a composition book and pen. Also, you need a quiet place and some uninterrupted time. I suggest fifteen minutes or more. If you think you may want to write a response to a scripture passage, you'll also need a Bible.

Be real. This is no opus magnum that will inspire—or be criticized by—others. This is prayer. If your internal editor springs forth with comments like, "Are you sure that's spelled right?," dismiss it with a reply such as, "Who cares? This is my journal." Also, a "hot pen" technique can help turn off the internal editor: Write rapidly with no thought as to whether this is the best way of saying what you're trying to say. No one else sees this except God, and God is always pleased with prayers, in whatever form they are expressed.

Just do it. I rarely journaled until I committed myself to do so during an eight-month Ignatian retreat (done in the midst of normal life). Before then, time expanses between journal entries stretched for months. This made me feel oppressed by how much I wanted to say. When I'd finally sit down to journal, I'd spend an hour or more writing page after page. Then I'd put off journaling again until I had at least a spare hour. Freedom came with a decision to limit myself to one page. I could go beyond that, of course, but my decision gave me permission to say just a bit and leave the rest for another time or for never.

Immediately after journaling, sit back and listen in silence. Give God a chance to respond to what you have said. Personally, I find this to be one of my most open times to hear from the Lord. A mental picture, a "still, small voice," a thought that gives me a new perspective, a scripture passage: These are some of the ways God communicates to me shortly after I finish a journal entry.

Finally, to keep your journal private, clearly mark it as such and store it where you can be free of concerns that someone might discover it and, without thinking, read it.

CHAPTER 10

Contemplative Prayer

My soul finds rest in God alone. (Ps 62:1 NIV)

Mona was angry with God. Her pastor and good friend had suddenly died of a coronary. Now here was this tall stranger, the new pastor, inviting any and everyone in the congregation to join him weekdays at 6:00 A.M. for thirty minutes of contemplative prayer. *No way am I going to do that*, thought Mona. *I have no time and, besides, I don't want to do it*. Even as these thoughts were going through her mind, however, her heart was drawing her to try out a type of prayer she knew nothing about. In the early morning light later that week, Mona found herself gathering with seven other parishioners and the pastor in order to pray.

Contemplative prayer is prayer beyond words, images, or thoughts—a prayer of being rather than of doing. One fourteenth-century mystic called it "the cloud of unknowing." Some call it "a gaze of faith." An elderly man in France conveyed its essence when asked what he did as he sat motionless in church every day: "I look at God, and God looks at me."[1]

This prayer form begins by quieting first the body, then the mind. To stop the storm of thoughts that invariably wash over the human brain when it is not focused on a task, teachers of contemplative prayer recommend devoutly and silently repeating a "sacred word" whenever the mind strays. Mona initially chose *Abba* but eventually discovered that the name of *Jesus* worked better. It enabled her to more readily become absorbed into prayer and, thus, into her relationship with God.

Challenges of Contemplative Prayer

Christian contemplation faces a unique obstacle: misunderstanding. Many shy away from this prayer form because they confuse it with non-Christian Eastern techniques such as transcendental meditation (TM). According to Father Thomas Keating, TM's goal is to arrive at an altered state of consciousness through repetition of a mantra/sacred word. In contemplative prayer the sacred word is used differently: to rid ourselves of mental distractions and surrender to God's action within us. In imitation of our Savior, we empty ourselves (Phil 2:7) so as to be more open to an infilling of the Holy Spirit.

A second challenge: Emotions and insights are rare during this type of prayer. What is asked of us instead is renunciation of self and a temporary suspension of our need for felt experiences of God. This is hard. Success in any type of prayer depends solely on the intent to be available to God. In contemplation, that's the norm. Our intent to pray is often the only way we know we're praying.

A third difficulty is distraction, common in any prayer but a challenge that asserts itself with amazing strength in contemplative prayer. "Be still, and know that I am God," says Psalm 46:10, but the brain resists. Finding stillness to be boring, the mind "races off to the future with planning and ideas. Or it retreats into the past to rerun old tapes and memories."[2]

In spite of these challenges, many find contemplative prayer to be wonderfully life giving; others do not. Experts say this is not a prayer for beginners, yet some beginners enter into it with ease. And many seasoned pray-ers say they cannot seem to pray this way. How can we determine whether this is a beneficial style of prayer for us? Primarily we look for results outside of daily prayer, not within it.

Benefits of Contemplative Prayer

More than most types of prayer, contemplation has a unique ability to reach levels beyond our ability to think, sense, or understand. God knew us before we were born (Ps 139), but we do not know ourselves. We need healing that extends beyond conscious needs and wounds. We need transformation. Contemplative prayer provides an avenue through which that can happen.

Mona experienced this benefit, finding healing in areas where she didn't even know she was wounded. The first healing was spiritual. "I came to believe I didn't initiate anything in my relationship with God," she says. "In prayer, I'm responding." This freed her from performance pressure, from feeling she had to say the right prayer with the right technique and with the right attitude. She could just be with God. The effect of this was a changed image of God, from that of a cold, distant judge with whom she was angry, to a recognition of God as a gentle, loving, caring presence.

Mona's spiritual healing gradually filtered into her other relationships and healed them in ways that mirrored the prayer form itself. "It freed me from having to do something," she says. "It allowed me to just be with other people. I no longer felt compelled to fix anyone or anything." It took a long time for Mona to recognize these benefits, but after six months of the 6:00 A.M. prayer times, Mona realized she simply felt freer. This, in turn, motivated her to keep on praying.

For You

Here is a five-step process recommended by Father Edward Hays:[3]

1. Sit still and quiet your body.
2. Consciously notice the act of breathing, letting it become slow, even, and deep. You may want to imagine yourself exhaling any negativity or concerns, then breathing in the breath of the Holy Spirit.
3. Let yourself be at rest. Typically, thoughts will wander through your mind at this time. When that happens, refocus on God by quietly saying a sacred word you have chosen to use (e.g., a name for God, a phrase from scripture, or a word such as *love*).
4. Go inward, silently repeating your sacred word. Don't let yourself be distressed by mental distractions. You'll be tempted to quit this prayer form if you berate yourself for your inability to stifle the flotsam of thoughts that inevitably drift through the human mind. Self-judgment will destroy inner stillness, and inner stillness is a core ingredient in contemplative prayer. Instead of internal warfare, simply turn back to your heart and to God's loving, albeit perhaps unfelt, presence.
5. Be at peace in God. How long you stay in this prayerful space is up to you. At first, you may find five minutes to be a stretch. A goal to strive for might be twenty minutes. Whatever time you establish, at the end of it let your mind gradually refocus on your surroundings, then close with a brief prayer of your choosing.

CHAPTER 11

Prayers of Music, Art, and Movement

You are my hiding place; you will protect me from trouble and surround me with songs of deliverance. (Ps 32:7 NIV)

Mandy's husband, Ben, loved his guns. Rifles, shotguns, pistols, he loved them all because they quieted some of the fear that had followed him home from the Vietnam War. But Vietnam had also left Ben with a rage that would erupt at the slightest irritation. "Sometimes he mistook me for the enemy," says Mandy. "I never knew what would suddenly turn him from a loving husband into a threatening tyrant."

The day arrived when Ben pulled out a rifle during one of his breakdowns. Mandy fled for her life, not knowing where she was going or what she should do next. She only knew she had to get away. Once Ben regained his senses, he felt remorse and pleaded with Mandy to return. She said she would do so under one condition: Get rid of the guns. "It's either the guns or me," she told him. "You decide." Ben chose the guns.

So Mandy found an apartment and filed for divorce. Now in place of feelings of danger came feelings of loss—loss of her home, loss of her marriage and, especially, loss of her dreams. Although surrounded by loving friends and caring professionals, she felt shipwrecked on a desert island. No one, including she herself, seemed able to reach her pain and ease it.

Then one night Mandy heard Vivaldi's "Four Seasons" symphony. At last came relief. "The music seemed to fill the room with compassion and a ray of hope," she says. "It entered into my pain and soothed it." Over the coming weeks and months, "I played the tape thousands of times...through my first depressing Christmas, my birthday, Easter, summer, and once again, fall. The music became like a friend who spoke to me of love and possibilities for my new life. It energized me to keep going."

Because Vivaldi's symphony does not appear in hymnals, it took Mandy a while to realize that the friend she had found was God, and he was speaking straight from his heart to hers. Through music, God was giving her the same message the Israelites heard when they, too, were in exile:

> The Lord's unfailing love and mercy still continue, fresh as the morning and sure as the sunrise. The Lord is all I have, and so in him I put my hope" (Lam 3:22–24 GNT)

Prayers of Music, Art, and Movement

The Gospel of John tells us that two thousand years ago "the Word became flesh and lived among us" (John 1:14). When we became flesh, God gave us the same senses that Jesus had: sight, sound, taste, smell, touch, and a kinesthetic sense of movement. Children use them with gusto. Draw, sing, clap hands, jump, help bake cookies: The list of life-giving ways to use the body starts big then slowly shrinks until, by the time adulthood arrives, much joy has been snuffed out because of the dulling of the senses.

Nowhere is sensory dulling more common than in prayer, which can narrow itself down to mental activity only. That makes healing more difficult because we are not disembodied spirits with disembodied needs. Rather, we are children of the Creator who gave us a body as well as a soul. This same Creator invites us to use our body in praying for healing. How we do that is up to us. Options include music, art, and movement.

Music

Music has the power to reach beyond the intellect into the deepest parts of our being. Sound enters our ears then seems to do an end-run around barricades that keep us broken and unhealed. As with Mandy, the gentleness of music can touch wounds that are unreachable by other means.

This type of prayer may be done simply by listening. Or it can be active, where we create the music by singing or playing an instrument.

Art

In 1996 Zoe and her husband were childless, in their mid-40s, and keenly aware of their ticking biological clock. That's why they were especially overjoyed when Zoe became pregnant. Months of layette creation and nursery preparation led up to the long-awaited time of delivery. But then, disaster: The baby was stillborn.

What can heal the broken heart of a parent who suffers this kind of loss? It's a wound beyond words. Therefore, prayer beyond words may help soothe the sorrow. Zoe found solace in sculpture, calligraphy, papier-mâché, and quilt making. "I needed to touch something," she says.

In the same way that music reaches our soul through hearing, art reaches it through sight and touch. Wounds heal when what we see and what we touch take on symbolic meaning: A sunrise speaks of new beginnings. A painting of Jesus on the cross tells us that we are not alone in our suffering. Words from the eighteenth chapter of Jeremiah come alive as we sculpt a lump of clay: God is the potter; we are the clay.

One source of healing for Zoe came from making a Tree of Life quilt for her stillborn son. Fabric textures and shapes helped her express her grief, see meaning in what had happened, and find a reason for going on with life. Insights came as she worked. For instance, a thunderbolt on the quilt showed her that for her, her son's death was like a bolt of lightning striking her family tree and killing the branch that represented her child. Images began in her mind, materialized into physical form, and helped Zoe move through her grief. "I stitched my life back together," she says, "one thread at a time, one day at a time." As her journey continues, she finds consolation and peace in a creative work—the quilt—that is tangible.

Art need not be religious in order to be sacred. Sometimes it is God-made: a sunset, a river, a mountain. Sometimes it is human-made by us or by someone else: a painting, a stained glass window, a manger scene, a quilt. Visible beauty leads us into healing experiences of the Invisible because we are visual people who need signs of God's presence in our lives.

Movement

Praying with the body through movement is surprisingly common. Kneeling is one example, where we speak to God with our legs as well as our mind. Standing, genuflecting, and bowing are other examples. "There is something you know when you bow," says Father Richard Rohr, "that you do not know when you do not bow."[1] He calls this a "body-knowing."

In 1998 I attended a sacred-dance retreat at a monastery in New Mexico. It began with people sharing why they had come. Some said they wanted to learn a new way of praying. Others

were seeking healing: A man had recently lost a daughter to sui-
cide; a woman needed emotional healing from childhood abuse;
another person was dealing with a physical illness.

So we danced. In myriad make-up-your-own-steps ways,
we danced in the morning, we danced in the afternoon, and, by
candlelight in a closing liturgy, we danced before the cross of
Christ. By the end of three days, I felt free to use my body for
worship. Now I often begin daily prayer by putting on a CD
and dancing. Sometimes I envision Jesus as my partner. Other
times I imagine I'm an infant in the arms of a gentle Father. Or
I see myself dancing before God's throne. There are no rules
and no critiques because this is a God-and-me event.

Walking a labyrinth is another example of prayer through
movement. A labyrinth is a large circular design where we enter
at the perimeter then slowly, prayerfully walk toward the center. In so doing, we move toward the center of our soul. Usually
created in the floor of a church or as part of an outdoor garden,
labyrinths are hard to find but are growing in popularity.

Melanie Bowden experienced the healing power of a
labyrinth when she was at a retreat center and seeking answers
to a family conflict. Initially reluctant, she decided to try this
form of prayer anyway:

> Within minutes, insight so overwhelmed my skepticism
> that I stopped in my tracks and gasped out loud. I'd
> found much more than understanding: A strong wave
> of forgiveness and sympathy also washed over me.[2]

People use labyrinths as a physical way of engaging in contemplative prayer. Father Rohr calls them a symbol of life:

> In a labyrinth you only have to make two decisions—to
> enter it and to stay on the path. If you enter it and if

you stay on the path, you will always get to the center....Stay in there. Stay in the life."[3]

Prayer Challenges

I see two main challenges to prayers of music, art, and movement. First is the ever-present temptation to be a critic rather than a pray-er. I can stand before a nativity scene and check out its artistic merit. Or I can allow myself to ponder the meaning of Christ's birth in my life, or imagine how Mary and Joseph may have felt in their homelessness and poverty, or visualize myself as one of the Magi or one of the shepherds. In other words, I can judge or I can pray. I can't do both.

The critic that evaluates someone else's work may mow us down when the offering is ours. We need to turn off this commentator that society has bestowed upon us. Healing does not come by judging the quality of what we have created. It comes by focusing on God.

Another challenge to these types of prayer is to recognize experiences of God as they occur. Healing through sight, sound, taste, smell, touch, and movement can occur anytime, anywhere, both during a prayer time and beyond. The key is openness to realizing that this is God communicating personally with us at this moment and inviting us to respond.

When something gives rise to feelings of awe, wonder, or peace, it's wise to assume that through this phenomenon, God may be reaching out to love us, to speak to us, to heal us. We need to extend our spiritual antennae and pay attention. As we do, we may be amazed to realize how often God communicates with us. I've heard God speak to me more often through sunrises than through homilies—and we have good homilies in our parish. Whenever I see beauty, I look beyond it to the Author of that beauty. God creates the visual or musical beauty, or helps me create it. I respond, then God responds back to me.

This is prayer. This is a personal relationship with God. Within that relationship is where we find healing.

For You

Regardless of artistic merit, anything you offer to God is a prayer. In addition to previously mentioned examples, here are some other ideas:

1. Draw or paint in journals, on easels, in the sand, or anywhere else.
2. Create a sculpture with clay or sand or some other material.
3. Do finger-painting. Wallow in colored goo—no symbols or actual pictures are needed.
4. Make a collage. Tear out pictures and let them speak to you as you arrange them.
5. Walk in the woods. Soak up the sights, sounds, and smells that surround you.
6. Bake bread. Talk to God as you knead it. Or think of places in scripture where bread is talked about. (This could result in many loaves of bread before you're done: In the Bible there are over three hundred references to bread.)
7. Sing in church. As your ears hear the words and notes, your breathing will become one with the music and with everyone else who is singing.
8. Sing in the shower. "Make a joyful noise to the LORD!" (Ps 100:1).
9. Play with a child. Nothing helps restore a sense of awe and wonder more quickly than to spend time playing with a child.
10. Work in the garden. When planting seeds, imagine that God is planting new life within you. Or when pruning

branches, reflect on Jesus' words in John 15:1–2: "I am the true vine, and my Father is the vinegrower....Every branch that bears fruit he prunes to make it bear more fruit."

The key to turning activities into prayer is to do them while directing the heart and mind toward God. Options are endless. Ask God to show you more and more of them so that you can grow in freedom to worship the Lord with your whole body, mind, and spirit.

Looking Ahead

We miss prayer's healing, transforming benefits if we can't fit it into our daily lives. The next chapter offers ideas for how to experience healing through our relationship with God while we continue to meet our daily responsibilities.

CHAPTER 12

The Prayer Journey

Devote yourselves to prayer, keeping alert in it with thanksgiving. (Col 4:2)

Many years ago a king dreamed that God appeared to him and said, "Ask what should I give you." What sounds like a once-upon-a-time fairy tale actually is an account of God speaking to Solomon in a dream (1 Kgs 3:5) and inviting him to ask for his heart's desire. God told Solomon that whatever he wanted, he would be given.

When we or our loved ones need healing, it's normal to wish for an experience like Solomon's: God appears like a genie from a bottle and says, "I'll give you whatever you want." Presumably the request is granted instantaneously. Sick one moment, healthy the next; depressed one minute, joyful the next. We ask, God gives.

We do ask and God does give, but the healing we seek comes in and through our relationship with the Lord. It requires daily contact with the One who heals. The question is: what, how, when, and where. This chapter covers these questions:

1. What prayer works best for healing?
2. How can daily prayer fit into a busy schedule?
3. When and where might we pray?
4. What experiences can we expect during daily prayer?

What Prayer Works Best for Healing?

A prayer myth described in chapter 4 claims that one type of prayer works best for all. Find it, do it daily, and healing will happen. Those who have experienced an earlier healing add fuel to this myth if they promote their own experience as a universal answer. "You're sick?," says one person. "You need to get into the Word of God. That's how I got healed." Meanwhile someone else says, "You need contemplative prayer. It will open you to deep healing." Conflicting advice like this leaves us confused and defeated before we even start praying.

A book, *Prayer and Temperament: Different Prayer Forms for Different Personality Types*, helps clear some of the fog surrounding this issue. After researching people's prayer experiences, the authors concluded:

> One of the great tragedies during the past several centuries is that we have been more or less forced by training into a form of prayer or spirituality that was indeed a proper method for one particular temperament. One was given the impression that this traditional method of prayer was the best method for everyone. When it did not work, the conclusion was that there was something wrong with the person rather than the method....Many good people gave up prayer altogether or went through the motions of praying without any real interior effect or benefit."[1]

Findings in *Prayer and Temperament* are based on prayer as it fits into the Myers-Briggs personality indicator. The authors learned that extroverts and introverts, intuitive and sensory people, thinking- and feeling-oriented people all experience profound benefits from prayer, but not from the same prayer form. Our God-given personality outside of prayer is also our God-given personality within prayer. So if we're feeling-oriented outside of prayer, we'll be feeling-oriented within prayer and will be attracted to prayer forms that enable us to experience God through our feelings. And if we're not feeling-oriented outside of prayer, then those prayers that focus on feelings will be a struggle.

In other words, the expression "different strokes for different folks" applies in prayer as much as elsewhere in life. It helps to know our personality type, but it's not essential. What is essential is being open to learning different prayer forms and then trying them out for a while. The authors of *Prayer and Temperament* found that 85 percent of the time we'll gravitate toward the type of prayer that fits our particular personality.[2]

So the answer to the question of what prayer works best for healing is: It depends on which prayer forms help us open our hearts and minds to God. That, in turn, depends on our God-given temperament.

How Can Daily Prayer Fit into a Busy Schedule?

Most of us who ask this question believe our problem is time. If only the day were thirty-six hours long, we'd have time for prayer. In fact, time is only a visible, felt reason for not praying. Two less-obvious reasons are boredom and a lack of awareness of prayer's benefits.

Boredom

Prayer that doesn't fit our personality feels as dry as dust and as beneficial as a wasteland. Finding prayer forms that match our temperament removes the tedium factor and draws us into prayer each day. It becomes a high priority because we experience it as being life-giving and healing.

Even a favorite prayer form becomes boring if we don't intersperse it with other forms. Like eating the same, mouth-watering dessert 365 days in a row, our spiritual taste buds get numb to the same prayers repeated daily, month-in and month-out. To "taste and see that the Lord is good" (Ps 34:8), it's important to vary our prayer "menu" and use a variety of options.

Lack of Awareness of Prayer's Benefits

One of my daughters quit going to church during her college years. Her decision didn't seem to be a conscious turning away from God. Instead, she would say, "I didn't have time to go today, Mom." One day I responded to her with a question: "If someone told you a million dollars awaited you, and all you had to do to collect it was go to church next Sunday and participate in worship, would you be able to fit it into your schedule?"

The same question might be asked about daily prayer: If someone said that a profound healing awaited us, and all we had to do to receive that healing was to sit down tomorrow and pray for twenty minutes, would we be able to fit it into our schedule?

Profound healing does happen through daily prayer. The problem is that it's rarely instant. Instead, the benefits of prayer are cumulative, like blessings received from a close friendship. God's normal way of healing is to give us tiny doses of it each day, doses that have a lasting effect because they're small enough for us to absorb into our being. These are easy to miss until we look back over a period of months or years. Then we see. Then we can say, "Wow, I've had a lot of healing since I started praying."

Making Prayer a Habit

Erma Bombeck once wrote that no energy exceeded her energy when she was avoiding a task. Putting off writing a column could stimulate her to clean her whole house. For me, no task consumes more energy than the task of deciding when to do something, especially if that "something" is a regularly occurring event. I can feel as though I've been exercising for hours when all I've been doing is spending hours thinking about exercising. My walking shoes are still in the closet, but I'm worn out.

For prayer to be healing and life-giving it must occur on a regular basis. Unless we live in the distraction-free environment of a monastery where the community gathers at regular intervals throughout the day, each of us has to carve out a block of time for prayer. Here, we face two options: a daily wrestling match, or a habit—an energy-draining decision that must be made each day, or a life-giving scheduled event that takes place at roughly the same time every day. One way to look at it is to commit ourselves to a daily "date" with God.

When and Where Might We Pray?

In 1973 I committed myself to daily prayer because I was very sick and no doctor could figure out what was wrong. For me, prayer was an act of desperation, not holiness. Over the years, I've wrestled with prayer's challenges, including the difficulties of figuring out when and where to fit it into my life. But twenty minutes a day with God, multiplied by thirty years has transformed my life. Spending a tiny amount of time each day opening my heart and mind to Christ has enabled me to receive more and more of the fullness of life God wants each of us to enjoy.

What follows are a few "when and where" ideas. Some are prayer forms that appeal to Christians from specific denominations (e.g., the rosary). Most ideas, however, fit into a broad spectrum of faith traditions.

- Reading the Bible when dining alone; journaling about it.

- Singing gospel songs (or other sacred music) while walking or driving.

- Listening to tapes while driving (e.g., New Testament, sacred music).

- Prayerfully reflecting in a natural setting, talking, and listening to God.

- Drawing about feelings or events.

- Making a pilgrimage to a holy site and praying there.

- Reflecting on stained-glass windows in a church.

- Praying the stations of the cross. (Outdoor ones are wonderful.)

- Meditating on scripture during lunch hour, perhaps in the car.

- Saying the rosary while driving, walking, when trying to fall asleep, etcetera.

- Reading religious materials (books, articles) just before retiring.

- Putting on a CD and dancing to it.

- Sitting in silence before God.

What Experiences Can We Expect During Daily Prayer?

Experiences during prayer are like a year's worth of weather: Depending on the day and the circumstances, we can feel hot or cold or just right; parched or satisfied; stormy and wind-tossed with feelings or filled with peace; barren of holy experiences or in touch with God's presence. What we want, of course, is summer without winter, lushness without rain, and growth without pain. What we get is normal prayer "weather."

Saints both living and from long ago have divided prayer experiences into two general categories: spiritual dryness (sometimes called "desolation") and spiritual consolation. The former feels lousy and the latter feels great.

Who wants desolation? No one. But we can expect a certain amount of dryness in our prayer times because God never wants prayer experiences to become more important than the Giver of those experiences. To persist in prayer despite periods of dryness is to say to God, "I'm not doing this just for my own healing or for warm feelings. I'm doing this because I love you and want to be in relationship with you. I'm here because you are here, even though I'm not experiencing your presence right now."

When we go through a period of desolation, the challenge is to discern its cause. Is it because we haven't found a prayer style that suits our personality? Or is it perhaps because we're shying away from being real with God during prayer? Or is a prayer myth the cause? Or is it because God is drawing us into deeper spiritual maturity, growth, and healing? Rarely is there an easy answer to these questions.

Experimenting with different prayer forms can help eliminate a prayer mismatch as the problem. Ultimately, however, we need more discernment than our own inner resources can give us. We need the support of others because even in the realm of personal prayer, we're not meant to be soloists. Always and everywhere, we need the wisdom and love of our spiritual brothers and sisters. That is the subject of part 3: Healing through the Support of Others.

Conclusion

At the close of these chapters on personal prayer, I am reminded of the fact that all the prayer forms and techniques in the world still leave us with one reality: Prayer is a mystery. We cannot control it because we cannot control God. In her book *Amazing Grace*, Kathleen Norris states it this way:

> Prayer stumbles over modern self-reliance, a…belief in our ability to set goals and attain them as quickly as possible. No wonder we have difficulty with prayer, for which the best "how-to" I know is from Psalm 46: "be still and know that I am God." This can happen in an instant; it can also constitute a life's work."[3]

For You

"To live, it is necessary to pray," said Pope Paul VI. The question is, what works best for you? And how can you find a way to stay with a prayer commitment? The following may help:

1. Looking at the prayer ideas mentioned in this chapter and in earlier ones, which of them have you ever tried?
2. What types of prayer have you tried that haven't been mentioned here?
3. Of the prayer ideas you've tried, which ones have you liked? Has one of them been especially useful for healing?
4. Of those prayer ideas you've tried, which ones have you not liked very much? (This may be due to their not

fitting your personality type, or it may be due to in-experience.)

5. Looking now at prayer ideas you haven't tried, which ones sound appealing to you? How and where might be the best place to learn them and try them out?

6. Finally, a prayer:

Creator God, Author and Giver of all that is good, thank you for the gift of prayer. Thank you for inviting every person on earth to come to you in prayer. Thank you that your invitation includes me.

I ask you, Lord, to give me the gift of desire for prayer. I ask for the gift of creative thinking, so as to help me discover my best times and ways to pray. Please give me the gift of self-acceptance in whatever prayers I do pray. And finally, please give me the gift of endurance in prayer. Thank you, Lord. Amen.

PART THREE

Healing through the Support of Others

CHAPTER 13

Ten Resources for Healing

It is not good that the man should be alone. (Gen 2:18)

The moment Dan felt the dull pain begin on the left side of his lower back, he knew the diagnosis: another kidney stone. He also knew the treatment options because he had suffered through each of them: another surgery or another retrieval procedure or another ultrasound zap in a large tank of water, followed by the torturous passing of many small stones.

Within hours, the dull pain had become a doubling-over agony that forced Dan into an emergency room. There a CAT scan and other tests revealed a 10-mm stone that was trying to force its way through a 1.5-mm passageway. The odds of getting rid of such a huge stone without medical intervention lay somewhere between zero and nonexistent.

Still ailing but on pain medication, Dan went home. On Sunday he dragged himself to church, where I met up with him. Seeing pain etched on his face and hearing his problem, I suggested that he and his wife and I find a quiet place to sit for a few minutes and pray for healing. The idea caught Dan by surprise, but he agreed to it. What was there to lose?

As the three of us began to pray, we did our best to focus on God rather than on Dan's kidney because this was prayer, not medical treatment. We thanked God for his presence with us, spent a few minutes in quiet praise of God's love and mercy, and then presented Dan's need to God. Dan's wife asked God to be the divine physician. I asked God to guide the doctors and give them gifts of wisdom. Then we entered into prayerful silence. The whole session lasted about fifteen minutes, after which I said I sensed that God was reassuring Dan and telling him to be at peace. There was no drama, no raising of voices, no sonic boom announcing a miracle. The three of us simply sensed a gentle love and peace in the room.

Perhaps the low-key nature of our prayer session added to everyone's astonishment over what happened in the next two days. During the rest of Sunday, Dan felt he was passing microscopic kidney stones, too small to see and barely big enough to feel. Then on Monday the urologist ran more tests to assess what needed to be done. No stone. There was a distended area where it had been, but the stone itself had vanished. "I don't believe it," said the radiologist. Neither he nor the urologist could figure out the cause of the disappearance, but the kidney stone was gone and has not resurfaced.

Do We Need the Support of Others?

America loves its stories of the hero who saves everyone and needs no one. On TV and radio, in movies and in print, the same message is proclaimed in one thousand forms: Strong people stand on their own two feet. They face their challenges alone and conquer them without the help of others.

Nothing in scripture or in real life supports this fantasy. "It is not good that the man should be alone" applies to each of us as much as it did to Adam. In good times we may forget this fact of life. The salary is rolling in, the jogging times are improving, the marriage looks healthy, and the EKG shows no blockage of coronary arteries. "I am the master of my fate."[1]

A broken leg or a broken marriage or a broken anything blows away this myth like dandelion seeds. When we need healing, the support of others is crucial if we aspire to anything higher than survival. To attempt to handle pain alone is to forget our interdependence with others, with God and with creation itself. So the answer to the question "Do we need support?" always is "yes." More difficult questions are, what kind of support? And who? And how do we find it? This chapter addresses the first question by describing ten resources for healing. It expands on material introduced in chapter 3, "Using All of God's Gifts." The next chapter then looks at who the appropriate helpers might be, how to find them, and how to participate in our own healing.

Support Options

The Medical Community

We all can nod our heads and say yes, yes, we need the medical community (both traditional and alternative), but it's hard to act on this belief in order to maintain our health. It's hard even when a need is obvious.

For instance, extreme pain from a kidney stone forced Dan to seek immediate care. More typical was his response to a heart attack that occurred at work several years earlier: Saying to himself that he "didn't want to bother anyone," he delayed doing anything for a while. When he finally did act, he refused to call 911. Instead, he left his desk, walked to his car with crushing chest pain, and drove himself to a hospital. Four days and one angioplasty later, he was able to go home.

Family

Family is a source of both death and resurrection. It's Good Friday and Easter woven into one tapestry of relationships. Our deepest wounds may arise from within the family, but so also may our greatest support.

The husband who holds his wife's hand as she goes through chemotherapy; the wife in a grocery store who holds her husband's hand for a different reason, because he has Alzheimer's and might get lost; the family that goes through the agony of an intervention with an addicted young adult; the widow whose surrogate family, her next-door neighbors, invite her to join them for holiday celebrations. Who can count the value of such support? It is priceless, and it comes to us through the gift of family.

Faith Community

The faith community is our extended family that gathers for worship, for growth in holiness, and for mutual support. It is here where we are most likely to encounter healing through the Body of Christ.

In addition to the large faith community that worships together on Sundays, every congregation/parish has numerous small ones such as outreach groups, pastoral councils, and the like, where everyone knows each other's lives. Here people can laugh, weep, pray, and rejoice together and be instruments of healing for one another. That was the case with Dan. From years of working with him in pastoral care, I knew he was comfortable with prayer and might welcome some ministry. His healing took place within a small faith community through the prayers of people who knew him well.

Friendship

"No medicine is more valuable..., none better suited to the cure of all our temporal ills than a friend to whom we may turn for consolation in time of trouble—and with whom we may share our happiness in time of joy."[2] How true! Friends love us, accept us as we are, and listen to us. They are good for the soul and, therefore, our overall health.

Jesus told his disciples, "I do not call you servants any longer...; but I have called you friends" (John 15:15). One of the many ways Christ's friendship comes to us is through human friendships.

Spiritual Companion/Prayer Partner

In "Companions for the Spiritual Journey,"[3] Father Leo Thomas said each of us needs at least one spiritual companion—a peer to help us stand back, see events objectively, and interpret those events through eyes of faith. This person also encourages us and helps us experience God's loving presence. The relationship is two-way: Each is a companion to the other. It's like a friendship that consciously includes God as a third, very important friend.

If spiritual companions choose to pray for each other's needs when they meet, then they also are prayer partners. My prayer partner and I meet every month or so, never knowing what each will bring to the session. We just know that by the time we've had lunch, talked about our lives, and then prayed for each other's needs, we feel peaceful and reassured. Over the years, each of us has experienced much emotional, spiritual, and relational healing as a result of our times together.

Spiritual Direction

Once upon a time spiritual directors were very direct. St. Teresa of Avila wrote her autobiography because her spiritual director (her confessor) ordered her to do so. St. Thérèse of Lisieux did likewise. Back then, to acquire a spiritual director was to become a child in the hands of a parent.

Today's directors are more like experienced guides rather than parents. Their primary role is to sit with us, listen to us with the mind and heart of Christ, then prayerfully help us see where God is in our lives and where God is calling us to go. They have the wisdom and training to be able to caution us when we veer into hazardous waters, and they can help us reflect and make life-giving choices. This is especially important if a need for healing presents us with dozens of options, all of them good. The choice then becomes not just what is good, but what is the greatest good.

Professional Counseling/Therapy

Someone once told me, "If I go to a counselor, he'll change who I am; then I won't be me any more." That's not what counselors and therapists do. Instead, they help us through "stuck points" in our lives. Going to a counselor is like calling a tow truck when our car gets bogged down in mud. The goal is for someone to help us out of the emotional, spiritual, or relational ditch we're in so we can get back on the road of life.

Support/Self-Help Groups

Long-term needs call for long-term support, and often the people who provide the best care are those who are facing a common issue. These days a support group exists for nearly every need. As noted in chapter 3, just discovering that we are not alone can promote healing because it removes isolation and, in so doing, increases hope.

Prayer Ministry

Dan's story characterizes prayer ministry: Two or more people gather to pray for one of them. They come before the Lord with a need, enter into gentle prayer, and present their need to God. Because the primary focus stays on God, prayer ministry is a form of worship. It is not medical care or counseling, which are entirely different types of support.

Prayer ministry isn't magic, and instant cures such as Dan's are rare. Nevertheless, something good always happens when we unite in prayer and bring our needs to God. For instance, three months after Dan's healing from a kidney stone, his earlier heart problem resurfaced as he began having exercise-induced chest pains. Tests revealed two blocked coronary arteries. So after Mass one Sunday, Dan, his wife, several other parishioners, and I gathered for prayer ministry—same location as before, with similar prayers. This time no instant cure took place, but Dan experienced a sense of acceptance and a feeling that everything was in God's hands.

Intercessory Prayer

As noted in chapter 7, intercessory prayer is a way to pray on someone else's behalf. One way to activate this type of support is via a prayer chain—a telephone chain where one person phones two others, and so on, until a large number of intercessors have been reached. The Internet has made the prayer chain even easier. One note to an entire address list can let everyone know of a need for healing.

When Dan began experiencing heart problems, he was asked if he would like us to contact a prayer chain. "Absolutely," he said. Within a day, thirty people on a prayer chain had been informed and were praying. And through an Internet-based prayer chain, forty additional people were reached.

So Many Choices

The ten options for support just described may feel over-whelming. What do we need, and when? One way to answer this is to break down the options into three areas: on-going support that's essential, on-going support that's desirable, and support for specific healing.

On-Going Support That Is Essential

Four support options are essential on an on-going basis because they help us choose life: medical care, family, faith community, and friendship. Without them we get sick in body, mind, or spirit. Yet busy lives can tempt us to put one or more of these on hold. "I'll have the eye doctor check me for glaucoma after I wrap up this project." "I'll spend time with the kids next month." "Sunday is my only morning to sleep in." "One of these days I'll have to phone Linda and see if we can walk around Green Lake together." Reasoning such as this, although understandable, eventually causes trouble because it removes us from sources of life and wholeness.

Besides helping us choose life, on-going support can come to our aid during an illness of body, mind, or spirit. Relationships built during noncrisis times can sustain us when an acute problem leaves us too dazed to ask for help. When we can't reach out to others, they can reach out to us.

On-Going Support That Is Desirable

A spiritual director and a spiritual companion/prayer partner are sources of God's grace and healing. They are hard to find, and those who do find them have been given treasures. I count myself greatly blessed to have a spiritual director and several spiritual companions. Again and again I have experienced healing through their love and wisdom.

Support for Specific Healing

Counseling, support groups, prayer ministry, and intercessory prayer are support options for healing when we have identified a specific need and are seeking help for it. They are for acute or chronic problems.

For You

These questions build on ones that were asked at the end of chapter 3. As you reflect on the following, you may want to refer to your answers from that chapter.

1. Consider each of the ten resources for healing that are covered in this chapter. Which ones have been sources for healing for you?
    Medical community (both traditional and alternative)
    Family
    Faith community
    Friendship
    Spiritual companion/prayer partner
    Spiritual direction
    Professional counseling/therapy
    Support/self-help groups
    Prayer ministry
    Intercessory prayer
2. Which resources have been the most helpful? The least helpful?
3. Which ones have you never tried or are reluctant to try?

4. Looking at the first four resources—those that are essential for maintaining health—how much support do you now receive from them (i.e., from family, friends, medical and faith communities)?
5. Which of the ten resources do you most want to expand contact with (or try for the first time)?
6. Finally, a prayer:

Lord God, thank you for all the healing that has occurred in my life through the help of others. Thank you for the love, compassion, and wisdom you give to those who support me. I especially thank you for the following people_____. Lord, please show me where I need continued support, and give me gifts of courage and discernment to reach out for that support. Lead the way, Lord. I will follow. Amen.

Conclusion: A Story

A man gets trapped in his house during a flood, but he prays and believes God will save him. As the water rises he's forced from the first floor to the second, then finally the roof. Rescuers come by in a boat and tell him to get in, but he says "No thanks. God will save me." The water keeps rising; people in another boat come and urge him to leave his roof, but he turns them down, too. Eventually, water is covering everything except the chimney. A helicopter comes and a rope is lowered for him to grab, but the man sends away these rescuers, too. Shortly after this, he drowns and goes to heaven where he meets God and says, "Why didn't you save me?" And God says, "I sent two boats and a helicopter. What more did you want?"

When we need healing God does send "boats and helicopters." Our challenge is to recognize them as resources for healing and then make use of them. To be healed through the support of others, getting into the boat or helicopter or whatever is a key part of the journey.

Just knowing the areas of resources available to us is not enough, however. We also must know the type of people to seek out within those resources. The next chapter looks at qualities of life-giving people, plus how to go about finding them and how to participate in the healing.

CHAPTER 14

Healing through the Support of Others

Are any among you sick? They should call for the elders of the church…. (Jas 5:14)

Back when James wrote his epistle, elders of the church
were a major resource for healing, a blessing that continues up
to the present. Now as well as then, however, not just any elder
or helper or whoever will do when we need healing. We must
find appropriate people. The wrong ones can leave us worse off
than before; the right ones can be sources of God's transforming grace. How do we choose? Carefully. With deliberation.
Not impulsively. And not from outside pressure. Here are six
traits to look for in those who offer us support:

1. *Love:* 1 Kings 19 relates a story about Elijah, where he
was told to prepare himself because the Lord would be passing
by the cave he was hiding in. Here's what happened next:

…[A] great and powerful wind tore the mountains
apart and shattered the rocks before the Lord, but the
Lord was not in the wind. After the wind there was an
earthquake, but the Lord was not in the earthquake.
After the earthquake came a fire, but the Lord was not
in the fire. And after the fire came a gentle whisper.

When Elijah heard it, he pulled his cloak over his face and went out and stood at the mouth of the cave. (1 Kgs 19:11b–13 NIV)

The power of God is not found in loud, forceful, earthquake-style ministry. Instead, God's healing comes to us through the power of love, a love as soft and gentle as the whispering sound Elijah heard.

Elijah hid his face in his cloak because the Israelites had been told they could not see the face of God and live. Then came the birth of Jesus, the face of God people could see. Not only did they see him and live, he saw them and touched them and they were healed.

The Lord's face still can be seen, this time in the Body of Christ—the people of God who reach out to us when we need them. The primary trait of effective helpers is love. Without it, Paul said he was nothing (1 Cor 13:2) and that remains true for all who support us. Without a foundation of love, healing rarely occurs. With love, miracles can happen.

2. *Compassion/empathy:* I once had a physician who was in such a hurry that he could have completed his appointments with me and still responded in a timely fashion to a fire drill. Compassion never entered the picture because his attention was focused not on me but on the clock and on my body parts.

Compassion means "suffer with." Compassionate people see our suffering and are willing to enter into it with us instead of trying to talk us out of it or give us advice. They see us, not just our problem. Their empathy helps relieve our isolation and fear, and that, in turn, opens us to healing. Compassionate people journey beside us, not above us or apart from us.

3. *An ability to listen deeply:* Whether it's medical, psycho-logical, or spiritual support, helpers must be able to listen to us deeply. Without that, they're reduced to guessing at our needs

and/or plugging their own agenda into our situation and coming up with a one-size-fits-all answer.

Father Leo Thomas called listening "a divine activity," and so it is. When someone listens to us in love, we experience God listening to us as well. And the better someone listens to us, the greater the chances we will receive appropriate care.

Effective listeners are warm, empathetic, and genuine. Plus (and this is crucial) they don't go blabbing our situation to others. "Three may keep a secret if two of them are dead," said Benjamin Franklin, but death is not necessary for private information to be kept private by good listeners. They know how to maintain confidentiality.[1]

4. *A personal relationship with Christ:* In spiritual areas, the people who support us need to have a deep relationship with Christ, one that has matured through the practice of their faith. This includes a personal prayer life and active participation in a faith community. Helpers without these practices lose touch with the One who heals. Then they lose their ability to bring God's life and wholeness to others.

5. *Knowledge and skill:* Beyond informal support offered us by friends and family, helpers need knowledge and skill. Enthusiasm and giftedness are not enough. Even Mozart had to take piano lessons. And even the Savior of the world had to "advance in wisdom" (Luke 2:52) before he was ready for public ministry. To avoid making innocent but hurtful mistakes, counselors, prayer ministers, and the like need training. The training may or may not include formal degrees; what is important is that it adds substance and experience to a helper's God-given gifts.

6. *A willingness to work with others:* After Dan's kidney stone was healed through prayer ministry (chapter 13), I asked him if he thought he would have experienced the same results by praying alone. He responded that as soon as he had felt the

first pains he had begun fervently praying for healing, but to no avail. It took the gifts of others, combined with his own gifts, in order for healing to occur.

A willingness to work with others is essential because even a powerfully gifted individual does not possess all that is needed for healing. Paul told the Corinthians, "There are varieties of gifts, but the same Spirit; to each is given the manifestation of the Spirit for the common good" (1 Cor 12:4, 7). When people unite in prayer or other forms of care, an increase of wisdom, giftedness, and strength is present. More healing occurs.

How Can We Find Help?

Celtic monks in the Middle Ages sometimes set out to sea in oarless boats to let wind and current take them wherever they were meant to go. Today when a need for healing presents itself and no instant answers appear, we may feel like those monks from the past: adrift and aimless. The cure for that aimless feeling is to respond to an invitation from Jesus:

> So I say to you, Ask, and it will be given you; search, and you will find; knock, and the door will be opened for you. For everyone who asks receives, and everyone who searches finds, and for everyone who knocks, the door will be opened. (Luke 11:9–10)

Jesus makes it sound easy but searching is hard work, and what we find may differ from what we expected. What does the task of searching entail? Where do we begin? The process includes prayer, action, and openness.

Prayer

Some people have a when-all-else-fails attitude toward prayer, turning to it as a last resort when all other options have failed and they're two gasps away from death. Personally, I see prayer as the best initial step in the healing process. Doctors, therapists, prayer ministers, and so on may be mystified at my suffering, but God never is. God knows specifically, precisely, exactly where I need healing and where I can find good resources. Therefore, I always begin the searching process by praying.

I keep my prayers simple and try not to tell God what to do. Instead, I lay a need before the Lord and say something like, "Lord, you understand this problem better than anyone in the world; you know the options for help that are out there. Help me find whatever I need. Show me the way."

From Prayer to Action

There's an expression that says God has an easier time steering a car that's moving than one that's parked at the curb. Occasionally, God does want us to park at the curb and wait. More commonly, he wants us to put prayer into action by looking for help.

Seeking can be impersonal: We go to the library, read articles, check websites, and so on. And it can be personal: We contact those we know and ask questions. Where have they found help? Could that work in this case? Is there anyone else who might know something about this topic?

Different people prefer different seeking styles. The introduction to this book told about Meg, who phoned me and asked, "Is there hope?" She was using a personal style of contacting me to see if I knew anyone who could help her. It happened that I did know a person with connections to an expert in complex dietary problems—one of Meg's many medical difficulties. A month after our first conversation, Meg phoned again to say that she had located the expert, had begun a special diet, and was feeling a lot better.

It's wise for action to include checking the credentials of those whose help we're considering. As noted earlier, beyond the informal support offered by friends and family, helpers need knowledge, skill, and training.

Openness

God offers us multiple resources for healing but never forces them on us. That's because free will is a sacred gift where, in effect, God says to each of us, "I will never force myself on you. I will never force fullness of life on you. Instead, I offer you myself every day through people, through scripture, through the beauty of creation and countless other ways. Be open. Say yes. If you choose to say no, I will respect your answer, but know that I will never leave you or forsake you. Every day I am with you. Every day I am offering you healing and life and wholeness. I am offering you myself."

In my experience, lack of openness is one of the most frequent blocks to healing. God offers us a full loaf of life. Too often, we settle for crumbs. Why? Because healing is work that usually involves a certain amount of physical, emotional, spiritual, and/or relational suffering. And it usually requires that we trust others to help us. This is risky business! M. Scott Peck describes it in *The Road Less Traveled*:

> Trust anybody and you may be hurt; depend on anyone and that one may let you down....Move out or grow in any dimension and pain as well as joy will be your reward. A full life will be full of pain. But the only alternative is not to live fully or not to live at all.[2]

Lack of trust occasionally reveals itself in not relying on anyone. More often it reveals itself in limiting our selection of resources: Medical care, yes; prayer ministry, no. Prayer ministry, yes; twelve-step program, no. Friendship, yes; counseling, no. A banquet—abundant life through abundant resources—is offered to us. Can we hear the invitation? If we hear the invitation, do we have the courage to say yes?

After Locating Help, What Then?

Locating help is like discovering a great restaurant. We've found something that looks good; now what are we going to do?

Getting Started

After locating help, it's good to keep in mind an African proverb: "Only a fool tests the depth of the water with both feet." It's wise to see if this particular person/resource is right for us. We may need counseling, for example, but some counselors are more skilled than others. Even among the best counselors, not all will be able to meet our needs and click with our personality and our situation. So a trial period of two or three counseling sessions or prayer ministry sessions or whatever, is good.

"First, do no harm" is a primary guideline for all helpers, but there's a difference between harming and hurting. The journey toward healing often pains us but should never damage us. One way to tell the difference is to use common sense and ask if this feels like the right resource for us. But the human brain naturally avoids pain and can confuse it with harm. So we also need to trust in the wisdom of friends, loved ones, and, perhaps, professionals to help us discern if we're on a path toward healing.

Eventually, we're going to have to take a bigger risk: We're going to have to fully enter into the waters of healing and life. How we do that is our choice. Some are dive-in-head-first people; others (such as myself) are play-it-safe, feet-first people.

Whatever the style, the important thing is to get into the water, get involved, participate.

Participation

Here's what I want whenever I need healing: I want to sit down with a bowl of hot, buttered popcorn and watch it happen. Let the good times roll while I observe my healing occur through a series of painless miracles.

Alas, healing is not a spectator sport. If we sit in the stands, little will happen on the field until we get down there and enter into the action. This is true whether the healing we seek is physical, emotional, spiritual, or relational. The help of others is vital; so is our participation.

Even in cases where a cure takes place all at once, a close look will show that almost always, the person who was cured participated in the event. For instance, in Dan's case he first said yes to prayer ministry, then he entered whole-heartedly into the session. He wasn't passive like a patient under anesthesia. He prayed with the team and was an active participant.

Many are unwilling to accept this reality. Faced with the prospect of hard work and a degree of suffering and lifestyle changes, they shop for a new doctor or a new pill or a miracle. Again and again in my work as a physical therapist and an active Christian, I have seen nonparticipation block healing as effectively as a brick wall. A patient with a shoulder injury learns exercises but never does them. A woman receiving prayer ministry becomes aware of deep-seated anger from her childhood then quits coming for ministry. A man on the verge of divorce refuses to attend AA meetings to deal with his drinking problem.

Every time I witness someone turn away from life and healing, I weep inside and think of Jesus' sadness when a rich young man turned down his invitation to become one of his disciples (Matt 19:16–22). And every time I witness someone courageously enter into their own healing, I feel a sense of awe. It's like being present at a birth, and in a very real sense it is: It is the birth of a much-loved child of God into greater fullness of life.

Conclusion

New life and wholeness are free in one sense because grace is free. In another sense, however, new life costs a great deal. It costs us our old selves, our old way of dealing with life. And it requires us to actively participate in the healing process. This is not easy. Many say no. With God's grace, including grace that comes to us through the support of others, we can be ones who choose to say yes.

For You

1. Think of the people who are supporting you in your healing process, then consider the following six traits to look for in helpers. Which people have some of these traits? Do any of your support people lack a trait that is particularly important for your healing?

   Love

   Compassion/empathy

   An ability to listen deeply

   In spiritual areas, a personal relationship with Christ

   Knowledge and skill

   A willingness to work with others

2. When you have sought support for healing, have you sought it through technical research? Or have you preferred the personal route of contacting those you know?

Or both? If you feel you need additional help, what avenues can you think of taking?

3. How well has healing through the support of others worked out for you so far? If there are ways it hasn't worked out, what options do you have right now?

4. In what ways are you already participating in your healing? If there are ways in which you have been holding back, what could inspire you to more active participation (e.g., switching to a different resource, praying for an increase in courage)?

5. Finally, here are several ideas for scripture meditations related to this chapter:

   Deuteronomy 30:19: "I have set before you life and death ....Choose life so that you and your descendants may live."

   John 5:1–14: The cure of the man at the pool of Bethesda
   Mark 2:1–12: The healing of the paralytic

Looking Ahead

The previous chapter explored ten resources for healing; this one expanded on the topic by looking at the people who offer us help. The next two chapters cover resources for healing through one's faith community: healing through Sunday worship and healing through anointing of the sick.

CHAPTER 15

Sunday Worship

There was a leper who came to [Jesus] and knelt before him, saying, "Lord, if you choose, you can make me clean." He stretched out his hand and touched him, saying, "I do choose. Be made clean!" Immediately his leprosy was cleansed. (Matt 8:2–3)

Two thousand years ago leprosy not only ravaged the body, it killed relationships because lepers lived apart from all except fellow sufferers. Worse, because the skin was thought to be a window to the soul, people with this disease were seen as horrible sinners. Rotten skin equaled a rotten soul that was displeasing to God. In short, lepers in the time of Jesus needed more than a dermatologist. They needed healing in body, mind, and spirit. They needed the touch of God.

Today we continue to need the touch of God when we are sick. As noted in chapter 11, experiences of the divine come to us through our senses of sight, sound, taste, smell, touch, and movement. These experiences can happen through sacraments that Jesus introduced during his time on earth. He himself was the ultimate sacrament to his first followers—God available in a seeable, hearable, touchable way. When he ascended to heaven after his resurrection, he did not leave us orphaned. Instead, he gave us the great gift of sacraments that come to us through the Body of Christ. God still is available to us in see-able, hearable, touchable ways:

> It is a central tenet of our faith that God can and does choose to enter into relationship with us through our physical existence, our very humanity. The celebration of the sacraments always involves our bodies. In the celebration(s) we are anointed, embraced, bathed and fed....We are invited to experience God's love reaching out to us through our senses."[1]

One place to experience God's love reaching out to us through our senses is at church on Sunday. Some faiths, such as the Catholic Church, call it Mass. Others call it Sunday service, Sunday celebration, or simply, worship. This chapter looks at what happens there and what is asked of us.[2]

Emmanuel: God with Us

What would happen if a pastor stood up one Sunday and said to his congregation, "Jesus will visit us next week! He'll actually be here!"? Besides TV film crews and perhaps a few psychiatrists interested in testing the sanity of the pastor, how many people would show up at church on the following Sunday? If Jesus came and touched people as he did two thousand years ago, would they experience healing? If so, what kind of healing would it be?

Actually, the Risen Christ does come to us whenever we assemble in community to worship the Lord. "Where two or three are gathered in my name, I am there among them," Jesus tells us (Matt 18:20). During every Sunday celebration our Savior and Healer reaches out to us as he did to the man with leprosy. He touches our ears as we hear scripture proclaimed. He touches our eyes, ears, and skin through contact with the faith community. He touches our tongues through the bread that comes down from heaven, as Jesus called himself. He also said, "The bread that I will give for the life of the world is my flesh" (John 6:51). That "life of the world" includes our lives; our healing; our wholeness of body, mind, spirit, and relationships.

Healing Benefits of Sunday Worship

Physical Benefits

Studies of those who attend weekly worship services show that regular attendees live longer than nonattendees—on average, seven years longer.[3] As of now, no one can explain why. All that's known is that healing of the human spirit apparently enhances healing of the body.

Emotional Benefits

Shared worship can bring emotional healing through the warmth and love of those around us. It can ease the pain of isolation. One woman, a widow, says when she sees people going forward to receive communion, she senses that each is suffering in some way. Each of them needs healing. Recognition helps her unite her sufferings with theirs. This lessens her pain because it moves her beyond her own loss. She becomes one with the suffering Body of Christ.

Spiritual Benefits

For his whole life a man named Andrew thought God had rejected him. This thought persisted until one Sunday when the opening hymn came from Isaiah 55:1 (NIV): "All you who are thirsty, come to the waters...."

As the music continued, Andrew became overwhelmed with feelings of God's acceptance. He sensed God issuing an open-arms invitation to be in relationship with him. Scripture and music came together during community worship and enabled Andrew to feel wanted and loved by God for the first time in his life.

Relational Benefits

When Cardinal Joseph Bernardin was dying of cancer, one topic he wrote about was relational healing:

> As important as the restoration of health is, it seems to me that an even more important kind of healing is the restoration of our relationships with God and with one another—being reconciled....It is at God's altar that we discover that we are all brothers and sisters, children of the same heavenly Father. It is there that we begin to strive to reconcile the disputes among the human family....Let us allow God's healing power to wash over us, cleanse us, and restore us to loving relationships with God and with one another."[4]

Three Essentials for Healing through Sunday Worship

As with healing through any other means, we need to take part in the grace that is offered us in worship. Three essentials are: showing up, expecting something good to happen, and participating fully.

Showing Up

In Luke 14, Jesus tells a parable about the kingdom of heaven:

> There was once a man who was giving a great feast to which he invited many people. When it was time for the

feast, he sent his servant to tell his guests, "Come, everything is ready!" But they all began, one after another, to make excuses. The first one told the servant, "I have bought a field and must go and look at it; please accept my apologies." Another one said, "I have just gotten married, and for that reason I cannot come." (Luke 14:16–20 GNT)

No one here was engaged in immoral behavior; each simply had something better to do than come to a party. Consumed with busyness, they missed a banquet. Today too, a feast awaits us every Sunday but many send their regrets. They miss much, including healing.

Some opt to stay away from the banquet of the Lord because of past hurts and present hard feelings toward the church in general or a faith community in particular. An awful incident or an awful person or a painful church issue keeps them from experiencing the Lord, and healing, through their community.

I grieve when I see this. And I recall what my spiritual director told me once when I was complaining about my imperfect parish. "The church is what it always has been—a collection of sinners. So what do you expect?" Oh, I forgot that, I thought. Now when I'm tempted to reject the church and, hence, my presence at Sunday worship, I remember my director's words: "We all are sinners. And church is where sinners come for healing."

Then there are those who stay home because their faith community's style of worship bothers them. The music distresses them or the sermons bore them or they don't like a liturgical change, or whatever. People in a very fragile state of mind or spirit may need to search for a faith community whose Sunday services best match their personality. The rest of us, however, may need the type of attitude adjustment I went through when I joined my current parish.

I had been attending church where the liturgy was one step short of heaven. Soaring music, stirring homilies, caring pastor, welcoming laity: This place had it all, and I loved it. Then one day I received a clear sense that God wanted me to leave paradise and join my neighborhood parish. My response? No way, Lord. With that, my spiritual life dried up. Music still soared, but my spirit did not. Homilies stirred all but me. Nothing touched my soul because, like Jonah, I had run the other way when God called.

Eventually a schedule conflict compelled me to start attending church at my neighborhood parish. The homily that first Sunday reached hitherto unexplored depths of tedium. As the priest droned on, I closed my eyes and sank in my pew until finally I prayed, "Lord, you have done me dirt. I can't stand this. Help!" Immediately a picture appeared in my mind's eye: The outside of the building was glowing with a blinding light, and God was saying, "I want this church to be a light on this hill, and I want you to be part of its rebirth." After the mental image came an insight: To the extent we go where God calls us, God will feed us, nurture us, heal us. It is our responsibility to go where God leads us and to participate in the life of the community; it is God's responsibility to meet our needs in that place.

Expecting Something Good to Happen

If healing is so available every week, why isn't it a frequent occurrence among those who do come to church? One reason may be low expectations.

I periodically serve as lector at Mass, a ministry that brings me face-to-face with the congregation. Sadly, when I look out at people, a number of them are sitting silent and glassy-eyed as others sing and Mass proceeds. I can't read minds, of course, but the body language of these people speaks of boredom and indifference. It brings to mind an expression: "Blessed are they who expect nothing, for they shall not be disappointed."

Expecting something good to happen is crucial for healing because it enables us to focus on God and on the good that is happening right now at this moment. We bring our needs and our very being to the Lord and lay them before the altar of God. Through all five of our senses, we are present to God through the Body of Christ.

To bring needs to Sunday worship, it helps to identify one or two of them during private prayer at home. We come before God as Bartimaeus came before Jesus and we say, "Have mercy on me!" Then Jesus asks the same question he addressed to Bartimaeus: "What do you want me to do for you?" (Mark 10:51). What is our answer? My own answer comes by focusing on some part of my body, mind, or spirit that is hurting. Then I pray for God's grace to touch me during Mass. If it's a deep pain, such as a broken relationship, I may bring the same hurt to God for weeks or even months.

The result of my prayers is that I leave home with the expectation that during my time at church, something good is going to happen to me. Some healing is going to occur. It may be small, but it will be healing.

Participating Fully

Having decided to show up at church, and having raised our expectations that something good is going to happen, we arrive at a third necessity: full participation.

Scripture gives many accounts of enthusiastic participation in worship, such as the story of David bringing the ark of the covenant into Jerusalem:

David accordingly went and, amid great rejoicing, brought the ark of God up from Obed-Edom's house to the City of David....David danced whirling around before Yahweh with all his might, wearing a linen loincloth. Thus with war cries and blasts on the horn, David and the entire House of Israel brought up the ark of Yahweh." (2 Sam 6:12, 14–15 NJB)

Three millennia later, war cries and linen loincloths are passé, but David's enthusiasm is not. The king of Israel worshiped God with his whole heart, mind, soul, and body, and we are invited to do likewise.

Full participation in worship includes greeting those around us as brothers and sisters in Christ. It includes listening to the scripture readings with the heart as well as the head, and doing likewise with the sermon. It includes singing hymns with zest even if those around us are lip-synching. Finally, it includes receiving communion with reverence and expectation. In the Catholic Mass, the last words we say before communion are "only say the word and I shall be healed." To pray this prayer in a heartfelt way is to give the Risen Lord permission to heal us through his Body and Blood.

Active participation benefits more than me, myself, and I because this is a sacrament for all. We do not go to church to have a private prayer time with the Lord, complete with musical accompaniment that suits our personal taste. We go to share community worship. We go to be blessed and to be a blessing to others. As others experience God through us, we experience God through them. Active participation moves us beyond a familiarity that can blind us to an amazing reality: The Risen Christ is truly present in this place.

Conclusion

Even when they don't label it healing, many people feel immensely blessed through Sunday worship. They say that through this sacrament, God meets a need within them that goes beyond words. One woman says she usually arrives at church exhausted from her hectic week. "I fall into the pew like a runner falling into the tape at the end of a race," she says. "By the end of Mass, I feel rejuvenated and alive."

"Rejuvenated and alive." That's what we want. And that's what can happen as we experience God during Sunday worship:

> What happens when I go to Mass and Communion? I realize my need. I get nourishment. I get healed. I become more loving. I find the strength I need. It sounds to me like a description of what happened when Jesus was alive. Hmmm...[5]

For You

1. Do you currently belong to a faith community?
   a. If not, what faith communities are available for you to join?
   b. If you do belong to a faith community, how would you describe it? Dry as dust? Marvelous? Some other description?
2. Consider your level of attendance at Sunday worship. How often do you attend? Why do you attend as frequently or as rarely as you do?
3. Each of us has expectations of others, including what we expect of community worship. Thoughts that are subconscious and unexpressed can hold us back until they're brought to light and looked at.

    a. What expectations do you have of your faith community's worship? How well—or poorly—are your expectations being met?

    b. How are you dealing with expectations that aren't being met? Are you enduring? Seething? Seeing the problems but loving the people anyway? Or are you now seeking another community?

4. When you go to church, how actively do you participate in worship? After reading this chapter, what idea(s) have come to mind as to where you might participate more fully?

5. Finally, what are a few of the blessings you have experienced through Sunday worship? What aspect of it touches you the most?

Looking Ahead

Healing through Sunday worship is only one of the ways to experience God through our faith community. The next chapter looks at another way it can be an instrument of God's healing: through anointing of the sick.

CHAPTER 16

Healing through the Anointing of the Sick

Are there any among you sick? They should call for the elders of the church and have them pray over them, anointing them with oil in the name of the Lord. (Jas 5:14–15)

The year was 1964, the patient was a mother of three young children, and she was expected to die within hours. In desperation, her husband phoned their parish priest and asked him to administer the sacrament of anointing of the sick to his wife. So the priest came to the hospital, applied blessed oil to the comatose woman, prayed over her, then left.

In *Healing Prayer* Barbara Shlemon describes what happened later:

I went off duty that night thinking we had instilled false hope in a hopeless case. The next afternoon found me back on duty. As I walked past the dying woman's room, I glanced in and froze in my tracks. She was sitting up at the side of the bed sipping soup. I couldn't believe it! The day nurse walking past me said, matter-of-factly, "She took a turn for the better last night."[1]

Many people "take a turn for the better" after the elders of their church pray over them, anointing them with oil in the name of the Lord. And when healing occurs, some people, including the elders themselves, are stunned. One priest was so shocked at a woman's immediate recovery that he fled from the scene. Asked later why he had run away, he explained that he just couldn't believe what had happened. It had scared him.

Anointing of the Sick: A Forgotten Grace

According to Morton Kelsey, nearly one-fifth of the gospels focus on Jesus' healing ministry.[2] And when Jesus empowered his disciples for ministry, sending them out in teams of two, they "anointed with oil many who were sick and cured them." (Mark 6:13)

Somewhere between the first and twentieth centuries, this type of ministry sank to the bottom of the church's list of priorities. Leaders (i.e., elders) continued Jesus' ministry of preaching and teaching, but responsibility for healing the sick slowly disappeared from their awareness. Over the course of eighteen hundred years, most people forgot that salvation includes the whole person, not just the soul. They forgot that Jesus cared about physical and mental health as well as conversion.

Rediscovery of healing ministry began about one hundred years ago, starting primarily with Pentecostals, then spreading to other Christian faiths. In the 1960s the Catholic Church's Vatican II Council restored anointing of the sick to its original place as a sacrament of healing rather than a preparation for death.[3] Today most leaders are working to bring anointing of the sick into the life of their faith communities. Many of us, however, struggle to know what this powerful grace is and how to use it. That is what this chapter covers.

Understanding the Anointing of the Sick

Chapter 13 describes ten resources for healing, one of which is prayer ministry. Anointing of the sick is a specific type of prayer ministry, administered by those whom James called "elders of the church." Some elders are ordained ministers; others are mature, committed lay Christians who have been elected by their faith community to the position of elder.

The focus of this type of ministry is healing from either an acute or chronic illness. Ideally it is a communal rite rather than isolated prayer:

> [Anointing of the sick] is supposed to be performed in the presence of people who know and care about the sick person....The church has come to recognize the importance of family, friends, and health care professionals for the well-being of people who are ill. Since they give so much support to the person who is ill, it is fitting that they join in praying for the person's recovery."[4]

Those are the basics. To truly know the power of the rite, however, it must be experienced. I recently turned to my parish to request anointing prior to major surgery. So after Mass one Sunday, family and friends joined our pastor to pray for me.

The priest began in silence as he laid his hands on my head. Then he prayed for healing and strength while anointing me with blessed oil. As he again laid his hands on my head and said a closing prayer, I felt an electric-type heat go through my body. That physical warmth became a warmth of love as family and friends each gave me a hug at the end of the ritual.

I would have rejoiced if anointing had resulted in an instant cure and cancellation of surgery. Instead, the heat I felt during the ritual seemed to be a strengthening for what lay ahead, plus a blessing for a remarkable recovery. Within a week of surgery I was able to slowly walk a mile. Within two weeks I was able to travel to a family event. The prayers of the faith community—both informal throughout my illness, and formal in this rite—gave me a lived experience of Isaiah 40:31 (GNT):

> Those who trust in the Lord for help will find their strength renewed. They will rise on wings like eagles; they will run and not get weary; they will walk and not grow weak.

Healing through Anointing of the Sick

As with any healing through others' support, to be healed through anointing of the sick we need to seek and find help, then participate in our own healing. First, however, comes the decision to be anointed.

I'm constantly amazed at how few people know about the healing power that awaits us through this ministry of the church. Some believe it's a deathbed ritual.[5] Others are confused as to when it's appropriate to ask to be anointed. Not wanting to be rebuffed or look ignorant, they do not seek help and, therefore, do not find it.

Seeking and Finding Help

Once we do decide to be anointed, we then need to look for one or more elders/leaders who know about anointing of the sick and value it as a ministry that's close to the heart of Jesus. This may not be easy. In churches where anointing of the sick is a sacrament, the rite is always available although sometimes done in a mechanical fashion.[6] In churches where this form of healing ministry is not seen as a sacrament, even a perfunctory anointing may be hard to find.

To the above challenges add the possibility that taking part in the rite or even being present for it might make some loved ones squirm. The result: Seeking and finding help may be the most difficult part of being healed through anointing of the sick.

Participating

Participating in anointing begins by contacting the minister(s) to schedule where and when it will occur. Then, if we want loved ones to be present, we extend an invitation to them.

Some ministers are accustomed to anointing in private. Others prefer a public ceremony, perhaps done communally where many are anointed in one ceremony. In my case, I wanted something between private and public. When I scheduled my anointing, one option the priest suggested was that it take place in front of the congregation during Mass. For me, that would have been too big and impersonal. So instead, he and I agreed on a time after Mass with just family and friends present.

After scheduling comes spiritual preparation. For about a week prior to my anointing I did this in prayer each morning. I asked God to help me expect something good to happen when I was anointed. I prayed for the ability to receive God's grace and healing.

Finally comes the rite itself, administered by one or more leaders with support by those present. I was surprised at how self-conscious I felt at the start of my anointing. Two dozen pairs of eyes were on me, and for a few moments I wanted to hide under the nearest pew. But once the rite began, I focused on the prayers being said, the hands being laid on me, the oil being placed on my forehead and on my hands, and finally, the loving embraces of those present. Leaving results up to God, I did my best to be vulnerable to whatever he had in mind for me.

Participating in healing through anointing continues through our prayers after the rite is over. It's tempting to try to analyze what occurred: A physical cure? An emotional strengthening? A spiritual healing? I find it best to skip the analysis and simply pray and remain open to God.

Conclusion

Life-giving surprises often await us during and after an anointing. A woman receives the grace to move beyond denial of her illness. A man feels his depression beginning to lift. Another man receives courage to deal with his fear of pain. Surprises such as these come to us in God's own time and God's own way. Our job is to say yes. God's job is to gently touch us through Christ present to us in our faith community.

For You

1. Does your faith community have a rite of anointing of the sick? If yes, who usually administers the rite?
2. If you have ever witnessed an anointing of the sick being administered by a church leader, what was it like?
   a. Do you know of any results from the anointing?
   b. In general, what are your thoughts or feelings about this ministry of the church?
3. If you have ever been anointed by "elders of the church" for healing, what was the experience like?
   a. What kind of healing were you seeking?
   b. Did you experience any results that you're aware of?
4. Do you think you could now benefit from an anointing for healing from an acute or chronic illness?
   a. If yes, what kind of illness is this?
   b. Which church leader(s) could you ask to do the anointing?

c. Who else, if anyone, would you like to invite to be present?

d. What concerns, if any, do you have about being anointed? Whom do you know who could address these concerns?

5. Finally, a prayer:

Lord God, Divine Healer, thank you that healing ministry is experiencing a rebirth in faith communities today. Thank you for leaders who now reach out to the sick to anoint them for healing. I ask you to continue to pour out your Spirit over this new yet ancient ministry of the church.

Show me, Lord, if I could benefit from being anointed for healing. If so, lead me to those who could minister to my needs. Give me gifts of openness and courage to reach out to others. Thank you, Lord. Amen.

PART FOUR

The Healing Journey: Walking with Christ

CHAPTER 17

Healing through God's Forgiveness

As far as the east is from the west, so far does God remove our sins from us. (Ps 103:12 GNT)

In Jean Shepherd's *In God We Trust: All Others Pay Cash*, a character named Ralph tells of years of torment at the hands of Grover Dill, a "yelling, wiry, malevolent, sneevily snively Bully" who finally decks his prey one time too often. Something snaps, and Ralph attacks Grover like "an unleashed Tasmanian Devil," pounding, smashing, and clawing, all the while screaming a torrent of obscenities. When adults finally pull the two apart, Ralph's mother takes him home, washes his face and makes him lie down.

Now the enormity of the crime dawns on Ralph. Worse yet: The enormity of the punishment he's sure to receive when his father gets home and learns what happened. At last...

I hear the car roar up the driveway and a wave of terror breaks over me, the terror that a kid feels when he knows that retribution is about to be meted out for something that he's been hiding forever—his rottenness. The basic rottenness has been uncovered, and now it's the Wrath of God, which you are not only going to get but which you deserve!"[1]

In the end, no punishment occurs because Ralph's mother covers for him. His dad never finds out. But how different this story is from the one Jesus told about another son: A man who demanded his inheritance, took off and lived a wild life, awoke to his dire need when his money ran out, repented of his actions, returned home, and was met by a father who welcomed him with open arms even though he knew his son's rotten deeds.

This chapter looks at God's forgiveness through the lens of the story of the prodigal son (Luke 15:11–32). When we sin, we don't have to quake in terror while waiting for the Wrath of God to strike us. But as with every avenue for healing, we must participate in this type of healing as well. What follows are four steps: recognizing we have done something wrong, repenting, reaching out to God, and receiving God's forgiveness.

Recognizing We Have Done Something Wrong

The prodigal son broke many of the Ten Commandments and probably his father's heart. But when hunger reduced him to longing for pig swill, he took the first step toward forgiveness. He admitted to himself that he'd done something wrong.

To be able to receive God's forgiveness we, too, must take this first step. Like the prodigal son, we must "come to our senses."

Repenting

When we repent, we decide we want to do something different with our future than what we've done with our past. Chapter 6 says that to repent is to change the direction in which we are seeking happiness. We turn away from sin and, instead, turn to God. That is what the prodigal son did: He left a foreign country and went home.

Repenting leads to new life because as we direct our heart and mind to God, we leave the foreign country of our false self and turn toward home—our true self.

Reaching Out to God

Recognizing wrongdoing and repenting of it does not complete the journey of God's forgiveness. Now we need to reach out to God. Some go through the first two steps but stumble over this one. Two reasons:

1. "I am undeserving": Some people shy away from God because they think they don't deserve forgiveness. The prodigal son expresses their feelings: "I am no longer worthy to be called your son." In fact, we who are human can never be worthy of forgiveness from the One who is divine. It is an act of mercy on God's part, not an act of deserving on our part; a sacred gift, not an earned wage. To wait to deserve God's forgiveness is to wait forever.

2. "I have committed the unforgivable sin": Some believe they have blasphemed against the Holy Spirit and, in so doing, have committed "the unforgivable sin." This belief tragically misinterprets a passage from Mark where Jesus says:

> People will be forgiven for their sins and whatever blasphemies they utter; but whoever blasphemes against the Holy Spirit can never have forgiveness, but is guilty of an eternal sin. (Mark 3:28–29)

Frankly, I wish Jesus had never said this because for two thousand years people have been asking what he meant. One opinion has burdened people with fear and despair by claiming that some sins automatically condemn the sinner to a living, eternal hell. Two examples:

1. "Anger at God is blaspheming the Holy Spirit." If true, then I'm doomed and so is nearly every Christian I know. "Be angry but do not sin," Paul tells us (Eph 4:26). In this I hear a call to an intimacy where we feel so safe we can let ourselves feel the full range of our emotions. When it comes to a relationship with our Creator and Savior, the God-given emotion of anger is part of the realness of that relationship. It is neither the iciness of estrangement nor the destructiveness of rage. Instead, it's an emotion that is part of a profound intimacy with the One we love.

But what if we do, at some point, turn away from God in a cold or hot fury? What then? The good news is that reconciliation is available because God never slams the door on a relationship with his children.

2. "Abortion is the unforgivable sin." I've seen this headline on tracts placed on my windshield. Those who work in postabortion ministry say it often is a woman's first statement when she seeks help: "I've committed the unforgivable sin."[2] She recognizes what she has done, regrets it deeply, and thinks God has rejected her forever. Her sin is bigger than God's grace. That's not true. According to St. Paul, sin need never have the last word in our life because "where sin increase(s), grace abound(s) all the more" (Rom 5:20). In other words, our souls are never broken beyond repair.

What, then, did Jesus mean by "blaspheming against the Holy Spirit"? Here's what the *Catechism of the Catholic Church* says:

> There are no limits to the mercy of God, but anyone who deliberately refuses to accept his mercy by repenting, rejects the forgiveness of his sins and the salvation offered by the Holy Spirit.[3]

"There are no limits to the mercy of God," but to refuse to admit a wrongdoing and repent of it is to refuse the gift of forgiveness. God will never force his gift on us. When we do choose to reach out for it, we arrive at the fourth step of God's forgiveness: receiving it.

Receiving God's Forgiveness

Here is where we can step into the scene of the prodigal son returning home to his father. We have come to our senses in a foreign land; we are sorry; with our huge or small sins we have walked home to our divine Parent. And now, like the father of the prodigal son, God runs to greet us, then embraces us and calls out to others to start a celebration because "this son of mine was dead and is alive again; he was lost and is found!"

Can there be any difficulties in receiving this joyous, all-encompassing love, a love without limits? I see three.

Experiencing Forgiveness Beyond Our Intellect

It's not enough to know God forgives us. We need to experience it as well. One way to do this is by confessing our wrongdoing to another person. Some may flee in horror at the mere thought of doing this. However, confession is common to most religions and to all twelve-step programs. Some faiths, such as Catholicism, treat it as a sacrament.[4]

Here's how twelve-step programs describe confession: "We admit to God, to ourselves, and to another human being the exact nature of our wrongs." The prodigal son did this with his father: "Father, I have sinned against heaven and before you. I am no longer worthy to be called your son." Having said that, he then could hear his father's words of welcome and receive his father's love.

The same thing happens to us in confession. We tell a loving person the ways in which we have not behaved as a child of God. We apologize to God—out loud—for falling short of who we want to be and were created to be. And then, like the prodigal son, we hear with our ears that God does not condemn us, but instead, forgives us. We experience God through a compassionate person who reaches out and says, "God has heard that you're sorry. God forgives you. God loves you." Not only do we get healed of our guilt; we get healed of our feelings of guilt.

Forgiving Ourselves

Sometimes guilt feelings persist even after we know God has forgiven us and has removed our sins. We may continue to gnaw on them and rehash them for months or even years. Why do we do this?

Maybe we think we must undo our sin: Unspeak some gossip, undo an adultery, undrive a car while drunk, unbreak a heart—then we'll forgive ourselves. Peter and Judas must have longed for this kind of reverse gear after they each betrayed Jesus and later repented. Peter wept bitterly but then moved forward. Judas, however, tried to turn back the clock by returning the thirty pieces of silver he had received for his betrayal. When the attempt failed, he hanged himself.

In self-forgiveness God asks us to give up what we wish we had done and, instead, move forward with our lives. This requires humility. Personally, I'm sometimes chagrined to discover that part of my regret for a wrongdoing arises from pride rather than humility. That was beneath who I am, I find myself thinking. Ouch. That's when I know I'm in need of forgiveness for pride as well as whatever wrong I've done.

Self-forgiveness humbles us. It leads us to say, "Lord, if you are willing to forgive me, then I am willing to forgive myself.

Rather than recycle my regrets over and over, I am willing to take responsibility for my past, make whatever amends I can, and move forward." Perhaps the size and details of our sins are huge. If so, we can say with St. Paul: "Christ Jesus came into the world to save sinners. I am the worst of them, but God was merciful to me" (1 Tim 1:15–16a GNT).

Finally, self-forgiveness includes accepting our character flaws while we work on them. When St. Paul's thorn in the flesh comes to us in the form of our own imperfections it keeps us from being "puffed up with pride" (2 Cor 12:7), but this is a painful experience. On a day when we've been especially irritable or impatient or opinionated or whatever, we may long to hide from God, from other people, and from ourselves. Yet God is always reaching out to us with unconditional, nonjudgmental love and forgiveness. Accepting that love and forgiveness frees us to move beyond the flaws we hate and the sins we lament.

Forgiving Others

Now comes a third obstacle to receiving God's forgiveness, and it may be the mother of all challenges: "Forgive us the wrongs we have done, as we forgive the wrongs that others have done us," we say in the Lord's Prayer. This is the two-way street of forgiveness. If we will not forgive others, it blocks our ability to receive God's forgiveness. We become like the prodigal son's older brother who, when invited to a celebration of forgiveness and new life, chose to remain outside. His brother had wronged him and he "was so angry that he would not go into the house." Even when his father begged him to come in, he refused. He wasn't about to forgive.

To receive God's forgiveness we need open hands and open arms. Nonforgiveness gives us clenched hands and crossed arms.

It blocks healing because it shackles us to our pain and to those who have wronged us. We need not stay that way, however. With God's grace, we can experience the freedom that comes from forgiveness of others. The next chapter deals with that topic.

Conclusion

When God confronts us with a sin, it never is with condemnation. Instead, he says to us, "See this mess? Let's clean it up." Then that's what we do. We cooperate as God removes our sin "as far as the east is from the west," and from that arises a glorious liberation of soul and spirit. This ripples out in healing ways to all our relationships. It empowers us to live the life we long to live. It brings us emotional health because now we know the truth: We are loved. We are forgiven.

For You

Note: What follows builds on the "For You" section at the end of chapter 6: "Prayer of Contrition." Before you consider the following, you may want to reflect on your prayer experience in that chapter, then look at the four steps of participation in God's forgiveness.

1. *Recognizing we have done something wrong.* After reading this chapter, do you see an area of your life where, like the prodigal son, you need to "come to your senses" (Luke 15:17)? If you're aware of a wrongdoing you would like God to forgive, what is it? (It helps to be specific.)
2. *Repenting.* Imagine that, like the prodigal son, you want a life that no longer includes the wrongdoing you've become aware of. Sit with your regret for a few minutes, then turn your heart and mind to God.

3. *Reaching out to God for forgiveness.*

    a. Have you ever thought you had to deserve God's forgiveness? If so, try to hand that belief over to God and, instead, ask for his mercy. (If this is impossible to do, you may want to discuss this with a minister.)

    b. Have you ever feared—or believed—that you had committed an "unforgivable sin"? If so, from where did this belief arise? What was the sin? After reading this chapter, has your understanding of this issue changed so that you feel freer to be yourself before God and to ask him for forgiveness? (If you continue to struggle with this, again, you may want to discuss this with a minister.)

    c. Imagine yourself reaching out to God with the wrongdoing you now repent of. Hand it over to God for forgiveness, and imagine God receiving it with mercy.

4. *Receiving God's forgiveness.*

    a. If you have ever confessed a wrongdoing to a minister or to some other trusted person, what was the experience like? How did you feel afterward? Think of a compassionate minister/friend/peer you might go to for confession, then consider turning to this person to receive God's forgiveness.

    b. Do you find it easier to accept God's forgiveness than to forgive yourself? If so, ask for the gift of self-forgiveness. Ask for the gift of letting go of what you regret and repent of, whether it's a past sin or an ongoing issue.

    c. The next chapter will deal with the challenge of healing through forgiveness of others.

5. Finally, a prayer:

God of mercy, thank you that you welcome all sinners, no matter what their sins. Thank you that nothing I do can ever cause you to reject me. Thank you that you long to forgive me even more than I long to be forgiven. I turn to you, Lord, and lay before you my wrongdoing. Specifically, I lay before you these things_____. I ask you, Lord, to remove any obstacles to my receiving your forgiveness for what I have done and what I have failed to do. Help me, God. Stay close beside me, Lord. Heal me through your forgiveness. Amen.

CHAPTER 18

Healing through Our Forgiveness of Others

Forgive us the wrongs we have done, as we forgive the wrongs that others have done us. (Matt 6:12 GNT)

On September 11, 2001, terrorists used four commercial airplanes to kill thousands of people when they leveled the World Trade Center, plunged into a field in Pennsylvania, and crashed into the Pentagon. Six years earlier, on April 19, 1995, Timothy McVeigh blew up the Murrah Building in Oklahoma City and, along with it, Julie Welch, age 23. Her father Bud, says, "From the moment I learned it was a bomb—a premeditated act of murder—that had killed Julie and 167 others, from babies in their cribs to old folks applying for their pensions, I survived on hate."[1] He also survived on chain smoking and alcohol until the day he asked himself a question: "How does revenge help me heal?" His answer: "It doesn't."[2]

It's one thing to know that hatred and vengeance do not help us heal. It's quite another to release those emotions and the events that caused them. Horrors like terrorism cry out for anything but forgiveness. Even placing that word side-by-side with evil sounds outrageous. Aren't there some sins that let us off the forgiveness hook? Terrorism would certainly qualify, as would abuse, betrayal, and a host of other sins. Isn't there an escape clause for ultra-terrible offenses?

Actually, no. For our peace of mind and healing, Jesus asks us to forgive those who have harmed us. But how can we forgive a hideous wrong? We may want to but feel unable. Or we may not want to but know we should. Or we may think we've forgiven but then find ourselves harboring unwanted malice. It can make us feel as helpless as the blind men who cried out to Jesus: "Lord, have mercy on us!" (Matt 20:30).

How can we experience healing through our forgiveness of others? A good place to start is to look at five myths about forgiveness.[3]

Myths about Forgiveness

Myth #1: When we've forgiven someone, we forget the wrong done to us.

Fact: Forgiveness does not give us amnesia. How can America ever forget the terrorist attacks in 2001 and 1995? How can victims' loved ones ever forget the atrocity inflicted on them? To do that, they and we would have to forget the people who died.

God doesn't ask us to forget the wrongs done to us because memory makes us who we are. We can never erase a deep hurt, but through forgiveness the horror of reliving it can cease.

Myth #2: Forgiveness is a decision.

Fact: Forgiveness is a process that includes many decisions. First there's a decision that sets us on our journey of forgiveness. The journey includes at least three phases: hurting, reacting to the hurt, and healing (described below). It's tempting to try to vault directly from hurting to healing, but this won't work. An injury resides not just in the hurting part of our being, but in the responding part as well. It dwells not just in our pain, but in the anger and rage that come after the pain.

After our initial decision to forgive, we face other ones as well (e.g., how far we're willing to go, how we want to forgive an offender, what we want to do about our relationship with that person). This isn't just one decision; it's many. And the more serious the wound, the longer it takes to heal. Emotional damage created by a serious wrong is like physical damage from a bad auto accident. Neither of them heals quickly. For deep and lasting healing, we must take our time and not feel guilty about doing so.

Myth #3: For us to forgive someone, the offender must apologize.

Fact: Forgiveness is possible even if wrongdoers never acknowledge the hurt they caused, and even if they aren't sorry. To wait for someone to be sorry is to place ourselves in that person's power. And who wants that?

> The person who hurt us should not be the person who decides whether or not we should recover from the pain he brought us. We should not be kept from healing by the muleheadedness of a heel who wounded and wronged us and will not even own up to it."[4]

For sure, forgiveness is tougher when wrongdoers express no sorrow for the harm they've caused. Before McVeigh was executed, Bud Welch said forgiveness would be a lot easier if McVeigh said he was sorry for what he had done. All that came was silence, a silence that again was heard on September 11, 2001. That does not mean victims' families and the American nation must be forever chained to unforgiveness. Evil can crush buildings and kill people, but it cannot destroy souls and keep us from healing.

Myth #4: Forgiveness lets an offender off the hook.

Fact: Forgiveness holds people accountable for their actions. Thinking about forgiving someone may feel as if we're going to say to that person, "You didn't mean to do it." Or, "I understand. You've been victimized, too." This would excuse a wrongdoing, and forgiveness is the opposite of excusing. With or without ever confronting an offender, forgiveness says, "I have been wronged, but I'm not going to let it ruin the rest of my life."

In criminal cases, we release accountability into the hands of the legal system, which may or may not lead to justice. That's why it's so liberating to also release accountability into God's hands. God is no fool. With the Author of justice, people like McVeigh and the September 11 terrorists eventually will not only recognize the wrong they have done but also will know the pain they have caused. This might not happen until the next life, but it will happen.

Myth #5: After we forgive someone, we must restore our relationship with that person.

Fact: Forgiveness and restoration of a relationship are separate issues. For restoration of a relationship to occur, a wrongdoer must bring an acknowledgment of the pain he or she has caused, plus a realistic promise that the hurt will not be repeated. In scripture, this occurred with the prodigal son. Admitting he had done something awful, he told his father he no longer deserved to be called his son. What if, instead, he had come home and demanded more money? Lack of repentance would have shut him off from his father's love and blocked restoration of their relationship.

Some people cannot keep a promise that a hurt will not be repeated. Others won't keep a promise. So while forgiveness is always God's Will, restoration of a relationship may or may not be. God asks us to forgive. He does not ask us to be victims.

Stages of Forgiveness

Once we have shed the common myths about forgiveness, we may be ready for the journey of forgiveness. This involves three stages: hurting, reacting to the hurt, and healing through forgiveness.

Stage One: Hurting

In the hurting stage of forgiveness we experience Christ's crucifixion. Bud Welch's began at 9:02 A.M. on April 19, 1995. Countless additional ones began on the morning of September 11, 2001. Ours may have started in childhood, or it may be recent. Abuse, a crime, a betrayal, a misuse of power: God does not expect us to excuse these horrors. Instead, he invites us to move toward forgiving them for our sake and the sake of those around us. Our other option is to stop at this first stage of hurting. If we do that, we remain frozen in place, trapped in a permanent nightmare.

Stage Two: Reacting to the Hurt

I happened to be writing this chapter when I learned of the attack on New York and Washington. Just as words about forgiveness were flowing through my fingers, my daughter phoned to tell me about the tragedy and its carnage. I felt as though I'd been slugged in the stomach. Pain, shock, dismay, sorrow: I experienced all these hurting sensations. Then when I hung up the phone, I said, "Kill bin Laden."

Reacting to a hurt often is felt as a desire for revenge: "He hurt me, I get to hurt him back." If it goes beyond an instinctive, first response to pain ("Kill bin Laden"), it becomes a soul sickness that can consume our life. Unless it is dealt with and healed, it eventually will destroy us.

Bud Welch lived in a valley of hate for six months until the day he stood in front of the bombed-out Murrah Building and realized his daughter would not recognize the embittered man he had become.

> Hate cut me off from Julie's way of love, from Julie herself. There in front of me, inside that cyclone fence, was what blind hate had brought about. The bombing... was supposed to avenge what McVeigh's obsessed mind believed was a government wrong. I knew something about obsession now, knew what brooding on a wrong can do to your heart."[5]

Releasing feelings like this begins when we start wanting to forgive someone, or we *want to* want to forgive a person. Like Bud Welch, we stand in front of a cyclone fence in our life and decide what we want to do with our pain. We can hold onto it, get even for it—as McVeigh tried to do with his pain—or move through it toward healing.

Stage Three: Healing through Forgiveness

Stage three in the forgiveness process requires much grace. A good place to start is to pray for the desire to forgive. Initially, we may have to do this through gritted teeth because the head usually precedes the heart: A decision to forgive often comes before the desire.

Healing includes draining off feelings such as hate, rage, anger, bitterness, resentment, and other unappealing emotions that leave a bad taste not in the mouth but in the heart and mind. If we find it impossible to get rid of these emotions, we may need healing of memories. Long-standing injuries such as childhood abuse may have damaged our identity and left us unable to sort out what happened, who we actually are, and where God was in the midst of chaos and darkness. Here, then, is where we need the support of others. Whether it's counselors or prayer ministers or a spiritual director or whoever, those who journey with us toward forgiveness need to be wise, gentle, patient, and able to accept the full range of our emotions, including rage and resentment.

Another way to open ourselves to God's healing grace is to do what Jesus said: "Pray for those who abuse you" (Luke 6:28). Pray for abusers? Pray for terrorists? The mind rebels. But when I took my willpower by the scruff of the neck and tried this after September 11, I found my prayers moving in the direction of asking God to bless today's terrorists with well-being and healing. That's when I saw that if a terrorist enters into a relationship with the One who never condones slaughter, he will turn away from evil and from any mission of being a human sacrifice for a madman. So, inadvertently, my prayers for killers ended up being prayers for America and for people everywhere. Also, these prayers showed me that it's impossible to pray for someone and, at the same time, hate him or her. Anger and even outrage about an offense is still possible, but hatred toward a person isn't.

The grace to forgive also can come in a powerful way when we put a wrongdoer into God's hands and say, "Lord, this no longer is an issue between this person and me. I now turn her over to you. You, God of love and justice, can deal with her better than I can. So I ask you to take over." This frees us of what some call a "trauma bond" between a wrongdoer and ourselves. Better yet, handing someone over to God gets us out of the way as regards God dealing with that person's need for conversion and healing.

The Struggle to Forgive

If forgiveness were easy, everyone would do it. Overnight, we all would be happier and the world would be a better place. Instead, this is one of the most difficult issues we encounter as Christians and as human beings. Why? Why is it such a struggle? I posed this question to several people who have experienced tragedy in their lives. Here are some of their thoughts:

"Denial is easier than forgiveness."

Carla was sexually abused by her father for more than ten years, an ordeal that traumatized her so much she couldn't bring herself to admit it had happened. Until she was able to see that she'd been hurt, there was nothing to forgive. End of story.

Some people recognize a deep hurt, feel guilty about their anger, say a forgiveness prayer, and think that takes care of it.

Neither of these solutions is the end of the story because with denial, nonforgiveness festers like a hidden infection that harms us internally, then surfaces in ways that puzzle us: Why am I having these headaches? Why am I depressed? Why am I angry all the time? In the short run, denial is easier than forgiveness. In the long run, it puts healing beyond our reach.

"Beneath the vengeance there's grief. And grief hurts more."

This is what Derek said a year after his son was beaten to death during an armed robbery. Bud Welch might identify with Derek's statement.

Vengeance feels strong, like an emotional fist in an offender's face. But beneath the vengeance lies a wellspring of grief that feels defenseless and agonizing. Having already been harmed by violence or injustice or betrayal or whatever, vulnerability is the last thing we want to feel. But if we're going to be healed and free, we must walk through grief's pain.

Self-righteousness.

I can easily slip into self-righteousness when someone harms me. "She done me wrong" asserts that another person is wrong, but it also implies that I am right. I am superior to my offender. In some cases this virtue-by-comparison only requires that I be better than a cad.

I now know this is a natural response to evil, but it leads nowhere. I've also learned that self-righteousness needs two people: the offender and the offended. "I'm right, she's wrong." "I'm good, he's bad." This ties me to the very person I want to be free of. It's an endless mental loop, and until I'm ready to exit from it, I remain trapped—walking like a conjoined twin with the person who has harmed me.

"As a victim, I'm not responsible for anything."

Robin succumbed to this belief after a date rape left her pregnant and a single mother. She says nonforgiveness became her ticket for blame: I'd be married if it weren't for him, she would think. I'd have a happy life if this hadn't happened. And, don't expect anything from me, God. She says when she reached middle age, she even found herself thinking that without the incident, her hair wouldn't be turning gray.

Forgiveness helps us see ourselves as responsible for what we do with our life. Yes, something bad has occurred and may even be on-going. But we have the power to open ourselves to healing. Instead of staying locked in anguish, we can make life-giving choices and move forward with God.

"It's hard to give up the victim role."

Valerie knows about the victim role because her father was an active alcoholic for decades before he gave up drinking. He spent his paychecks on alcohol, flew into rages, beat Valerie's mother, and petrified the family with threats. Once he went into a closet with a shotgun, said he was going to kill himself, then fired the gun into the ceiling. Expecting to find a mutilated body, his children opened the closet door in a state of terror. There was their father, still drunk, still angry, still blaming them for all his problems.

Valerie says being victimized felt terrible, not just because of the damage done, but because it left her feeling powerless. Eventually she realized she had two choices: the way of the world or the way of Jesus.

In the world's way, being victimized expands from an event or a relationship until it becomes our identity. God's way offers Jesus as a role model. Through his crucifixion he showed us how to be a victim. He forgave his executioners rather than soak up the hatred surrounding him on Calvary. He trusted in God's power to bring victory out of disaster. Rather than adopt the victim role as a way of life, he rose from the dead.

We, too, can rise from the dead if we allow God to transform our heart. Valerie struggled with this because letting go of the victim role felt like dying. It felt as though "Victim" was a permanent name tag—who she really was—and now God wanted her to give that up.

God wants us to give up the victim role and move toward forgiveness. If we do that, we'll probably discover two things that Robin and Valerie both learned: First, forgiveness will turn our focus away from someone else's shortcomings and onto our own. Initially this does not feel good. But eventually it frees us to be who we really want to be.

Second, Robin and Valerie discovered that wounds don't usually bring out the best in us. If we've been harboring the negative emotions of a victim, almost invariably we pass that pain on to others. Intending to harm only the guilty, we often injure the innocent as well because bitterness, resentment, and so on, are not "smart bombs." They're more like poison gas.

Benefits of Forgiving Others

1. *It frees us from those who have hurt us.* We are liberated from the shackles of a wrongdoer. The offender no longer dwells inside us, exerting power over us.

2. *It opens us to God and, therefore, to healing.* The healing may be physical, such as the disappearance of migraine headaches. It may be emotional, such as the easing of clinical depression. Certainly it will be spiritual because forgiveness is a type of spiritual healing. And often there is relational healing in the aftermath of our forgiveness of someone.

3. *Forgiveness makes us more like Christ.* Eventually Bud Welch reached the point where he opposed McVeigh's execution. "I think even dastardly criminals have souls that should be saved," he said. "As long as there's life, there's a chance."[6] Human willpower alone could not create so much largeness of heart. It was a work of God that has made Welch more like Christ, more like his daughter, less like McVeigh.

4. *With forgiveness, the energy of bitterness changes into the energy of positive action.* As bitterness fades, what emerges is strength to do good for the sake of others. We have more life, and that life spills out to others.

5. *Forgiving others opens us to being able to receive God's forgiveness of us.* Here is where words from the Lord's Prayer come to life for us: "Forgive us the wrongs we have done, as we forgive the wrongs that others have done us." When we forgive

others, not only do we become free of tormenters beyond ourselves, but also we become free of the sin within.

6. *Through forgiveness we can discover who we really are.* We're not a victim, but a person; not a powerless child, but a child of God who is capable of moving beyond the past into a future full of hope.

Conclusion

"Forgiveness is love's toughest task and love's biggest risk," says Lewis Smedes. Just as I've never met anyone with perfect love, so too I've never met anyone with perfect forgiveness. Even experts are amateurs, and I, a nonexpert, am a beginner. What does God ask of us? I believe he wants us to begin and then keep going. "Love your enemies," says Jesus (Luke 6:27). I haven't arrived at this point yet, but I'm moving toward the goal. Here's how Bishop George Thomas expressed my efforts, and the efforts of many, three days after the terrorist attacks on September 11:

> We struggle with the words and example of Jesus Christ who told his disciples, "Love your enemies, do good to those who hate you; bless those who curse you, and pray for those who maltreat you." Left to our own devices, we realize that we fall short—painfully short— of our Master's mandate. Only by God's own grace can we muster the strength to pray for our enemies and ask our good and gracious God to remove the roots of violence and hatred from every human heart."[7]

For You

1. Consider the five myths described in this chapter and ask yourself how many of them you have believed in the

past. After reading this chapter, have any of those beliefs changed?

2. Think of someone who has harmed you in the past or present:
   a. Who was this person and how serious was the harm?
   b. If you've attempted to forgive this person, how successful do you think your effort has been?
   c. If you used outside resources for help in forgiving this person, what were those resources? How helpful were they?

3. Someone once said nonforgiveness is like drinking poison and expecting the other person to die. If you've ever refused or felt unable to forgive someone who's hurt you, what kind of impact has this had on your life? Your health? Your relationship with God? Your relationship with others?

4. In closing, a prayer:

God of love, God of forgiveness and mercy, thank you for all the times and ways you have forgiven me. Help me, Lord, to imitate you. Please give me the gift of wanting to forgive those who have hurt me. Specifically, I bring before you one person: _____. Walk beside me and help me forgive him/her. Help me face feelings I do not want to have. Give me the grace to forgive. Heal me, Lord, so that I can be more like you. Amen.

CHAPTER 19

Healing in the Midst of a Serious Illness

In the world you will have suffering. But take heart! I
have conquered the world. (John 16:33 REB)

In *Traveling Mercies*, Anne Lamott tells of a neighbor who
learns he has lung cancer that has spread to his brain. Anne
watches Rick go through vast treatments while remaining
upbeat and cheerful. This astounds Anne, who says a head cold
flattens her more than any surgery, chemotherapy, radiation, or
alternative therapy has crushed Rick. The reason for this eludes
her until she reads an article where an interviewer asks Rick
how he copes:

> He said that he's so savoring the moments of his life
> right now, so acutely aware of love and small pleasures
> that he no longer feels he has a life-threatening disease;
> he now says he's leading a disease-threatening life."[1]

Jesus tells us "in the world you will have suffering." He
doesn't say, "If you're unlucky, you'll suffer," or "If you're bad,
you'll suffer." He says we will have suffering. The question is,
how do we "take heart" and experience healing in the midst of
it? How do we "live a disease-threatening life" like Rick? This
chapter addresses these questions.

Kinds of Serious Illnesses

Here's a typical scenario: Life is rolling along in ho-hum fashion and yes, we sort of appreciate it. But hassles annoy us and things periodically get boring until—boom!—along comes a cancer diagnosis, or an accident, or a marital infidelity, or the death of a loved one, or....Now everything gets turned upside down and inside out. Now we are eyeball-to-eyeball with something major, a "something" that might include any of the following:

- Physical illness such as cancer.

- Emotional illness (e.g, grief, posttraumatic stress, or mental illness).

- Spiritual illness (e.g., an addiction to alcohol).

- Relational illness such as divorce.

- Acute illness/trauma arising from a heart attack or an accident.

- Chronic illness such as multiple sclerosis.

- Illness/disability that remains fairly stable (e.g., a spinal cord injury).

- Illness/disability that worsens with time (e.g., Parkinson's disease).

The above labels do not matter so much as the havoc and anguish they cause. Whether it's physical, emotional, spiritual, or relational; acute or chronic; stable or deteriorating, what matters is that something terrible happens to us or a loved one. It stops us cold, shatters our life, consumes our waking moments, and sometimes leaves us in a pit of despair. Our challenge is to experience healing at these times and in these circumstances. How we respond to suffering has a big impact on that.

Responding to Suffering

A story: Joe lives in a house that's a wreck. Fire has gutted the family room, several windows are boarded up, tumbleweed-size dust balls roll through the rooms, and the lawn could be declared a national monument because of its "tall prairie grass" status. One day Joe receives a letter from Jesus saying that he would like to live with him and hopes he likes this idea. Joe loves the idea, but he hates his house. So when Jesus arrives on the doorstep a few days later, the house is there but Joe isn't. He's a few miles down the road, sitting in a model home in a new development. He's looking forward to Jesus' appearance with great excitement, but Jesus hasn't gone to the model home. He's back at Joe's house, waiting for him to return.

St. Paul said we are a temple of God, and God's Spirit dwells in us (1 Cor 3:16). Illness can make our temple feel like Joe's house: broken, dusty, and gutted. We hate living there, and the thought of Jesus living there with us makes us shudder. So here's what many of us do for at least a while: We mentally, emotionally, and/or spiritually leave the "house" of reality. We go elsewhere: into the past we once had or wanted to have, into the future we'll have after Jesus heals us, into a fantasy of life as we want it to be, into anything but this life with this illness.

These "elsewheres" block healing and may even kill us. To be healed by Jesus, we must live where he lives: in the body, mind, spirit, and relationships we have today, in the wounds we suffer from right now. Jesus asks us to be here in our broken-ness, in reality.

Being in the Reality of an Illness

Acute Illness

A second story: A woman falls down and breaks her femur. It's so angled that she looks like she's acquired a new joint in the middle of her thigh. Medics arrive, ready to take the woman to the hospital, but she staggers up onto her one good leg and says, "Thanks, but I don't have time to deal with this. I've got three meetings scheduled today, and tomorrow my son graduates from college. Then I've got to do this, and this, and this...." So off the woman goes, gasping with pain as she grinds her femur into shards.

That's crazy, of course, because a broken leg or an auto accident seizes our attention. It says, "Stop everything. Move this to the top of any list you have. You must deal with this now." If all acute problems were as obvious as fractures, cure rates would soar. Unfortunately, illnesses such as cancer may be just as acute but far more subtle. A broken bone shouts, cancer symptoms whisper. They both say, "deal with this now," but in the face of a suspicious lump or strange bleeding, it's easy to dodge reality by leaving the "house" of an ailing body.

A third story, this one true: While taking a shower one morning, Liz finds what every woman dreads: a lump in her breast. At first she ignores it because she's about to leave on a once-in-a-lifetime trip. She tells herself she'll call the doctor when she gets back. But now a friend discovers she has breast cancer. This shocks Liz into leaving the dream of her future trip and facing the unwanted fact of a lump. She goes to her doctor and learns that yes, she has cancer and it has already spread to several lymph nodes. However, it turns out to be curable with aggressive treatment. If she had delayed seeing a doctor until later, more than her trip would have been over; her life would have been over as well.

Healing from an acute illness requires us to give it our undivided attention for a period of time. Getting well becomes a full-time job that may include a leave of absence from our career. Here's where we tap into the ten resources for healing described in chapter 13: medicine, family support, faith community, intercessory prayer, and so on. In Liz's case, the job of healing included doctor appointments, medical tests, surgery, chemotherapy, follow-up care, counseling, and prayer ministry—six months of concentration on an illness. Seven years later, Liz says the time and pain were worth it. She is alive, cancer-free, and grateful for each day.

Chronic Illness/Disability

In gospel accounts of Jesus healing the sick, some, such as Lazarus, had an acute illness. Most, however, had a chronic illness or disability. Paralysis, blindness, deafness, leprosy, epilepsy: All these and more created a desperation that led people to hunt Jesus down and beg him to heal them.

Chronic illnesses create the same desperation today because they have no time limit. With an acute problem we can buck up and take heart by telling ourselves this will pass; life will eventually return to normal. We can't say that about a chronic problem. Instead, the future stretches before us in an unbroken vision of brokenness.

Another difference between acute and chronic illnesses: With an acute illness, we direct our full attention to it for a while, whereas with a chronic illness we do the opposite: We go on with life while we deal with our problem. We balance two realities: our on-going illness and our on-going life. This balance is not easy to achieve.

Some people refuse to accommodate their illness and, instead, ignore it. They forge ahead with the life they want rather than the life they have. Invariably, this harms them and their loved ones. For instance, a woman with diabetes who brushes off the importance of controlling her blood sugar will injure her body, shorten her life, and grieve her family.

At the other end of the spectrum of not accommodating a chronic illness are those who let it hold them back. Molly was an example of this: Every year she flew three thousand miles to visit her family in Seattle. Unfortunately, she had emphysema that worsened with time until finally one year, she had to be pushed in a wheelchair through two airport terminals. This mortified Molly and wounded her pride, to the point where she said she never would travel again. So she didn't. She lived eight more years without ever again leaving her hometown. Her Seattle relatives couldn't afford many trips, so she rarely saw them. By refusing to use a wheelchair in airport terminals, Molly let emphysema rule her life and rob her of joy.

I've been coping with a chronic disease since 1973, but I am more than an illness with arms, legs, head, and trunk. I never introduce myself by saying, "Hi, I'm Jan. I'm an illness." However, I sometimes get anxious and depressed when my disease flares up. My challenge is to move beyond my mood, deal with my problem, and live the life I have. It helps when I recall a prayer experience I once had:

> In my mind's eye, I saw two pictures simultaneously, like a split picture on a TV screen. One picture was a sunny rose garden with a level path winding through groomed flower beds. The other picture was a mountainous landscape above timberline. It featured drizzle, rocks, scrawny plants, and a steep, rocky path that disappeared into grayness beyond a trailhead. It

also featured Jesus, standing at the trailhead and inviting me to choose either of the two paths. I chose the rocky path because that's where Jesus was. How could I have chosen the rose garden? It was an outdoor version of the model home Joe wanted, and Jesus wasn't there.

An entire book of the Bible was written for those who walk the rocky path of a chronic illness: the Book of Job. Here's a man who suffers the loss of his family (relational wound), then his health (physical wound). He sinks into depression (emotional wound) and enters into a crisis of faith (spiritual wound). As if that weren't enough, Job has what most other sufferers have: advice givers. They tell Job it's his fault that he's sick: "It is man who breeds trouble for himself as surely as eagles fly to the height." (Job 5:7 JB) They tell him what to do (confess his sins) and how to do it. They've figured out what's wrong, and they don't hold back on telling him all about it.

Job's friends live on in the twenty-first century, handing out unasked-for advice while thinking they're being helpful. Over the years I've been urged to use every medical and natural remedy known to humankind. And in the area of spiritual answers, people who don't even know my name have told me that, (1) I need to confess some as-yet-unforgiven sin, or (2) I'm sick because I don't have the faith to be healed, or (3) I should "claim my healing" and stop taking my medicine. I've also been told that my illness is God's Will—a belief that puts God into the role of an abusive parent who inflicts disease and harm upon his helpless children. It's an opinion that contradicts everything Jesus said and did in his healing ministry.

God does not want us to be sick, yet sometimes we are. Jesus says he has conquered the world, but sometimes it feels as though he's conquered nothing. The reality of a rocky path clashes with the fullness of life Jesus came to bring us. I once thought that fullness would look like the rose garden in my prayer vision. I not only wanted that garden; I expected it as I sought a happily-ever-after life of adventure, comfort, and approval. Through illness, what I got instead was a kind of richness I didn't know existed: a relationship with God, emotional and spiritual healing, a compassion for those in pain, and a writing ministry.

In losing my dream of what I thought life would be like, I gained something better, but it has taken a long time to see the gain. And my illness still sometimes depresses, frustrates, and angers me. At those times, the words of an old song come to me: "I beg your pardon; I never promised you a rose garden." "Very funny," I say to Jesus, while at the same time admitting that I freely chose the rocky path, not the rose garden.

"Taking Heart"

So how do we "take heart" as Jesus urged, while also accepting that we will suffer during our life? A serious illness pulls us into a mystery beyond answers. What follows, therefore, aren't answers but instead are quotes and thoughts that have helped me:

1. "Yesterday is gone. Tomorrow has not yet come. We have only today. Let us begin" (Mother Teresa). Living with an illness in the present moment is the basis for the healing of that illness. When we begin—when we're able say, "This is the life I have today, and I'm going to deal with it"—we open ourselves to God's grace. We may or may not experience the particular healing we seek but, for certain, God will touch us and transform us.

2. "Only grief permits newness" (Walter Brueggemann). As we live in the present, we encounter feelings of what we

wanted life to be. A shattered marriage, the death of a loved one, paralysis: Wounds like these are huge losses, and we need to grieve them before we can accept them. (This topic is explored in the next chapter: "From Good Friday to Pentecost and Beyond.")

3. "Keep returning to those to whom you belong and who keep you in the light" (Henri Nouwen).[2] Chapters 13 and 14 describe the importance of quality support—not the kind of advice-giving that Job endured, but the support of those who "keep us in the light" and help us on our journey.

4. "Proceed as the way opens" (William Least Heat-Moon).[3] This was Heat-Moon's motto for a 5,200 mile trip across America in a small boat. En route, he and his copilot encountered hundreds of watery road blocks: massive floods, inoperative canal locks, submerged rocks, high winds, plus their own doubts and, yes, fear. Every time they wondered what to do, they repeated their motto to each other: "Proceed as the way opens."

Invariably a serious illness brings us into contact with obstacles and turbulence. When that happens, our normal response will be similar to the disciples during a storm on the Sea of Galilee. Our boat of life is about to sink, and Jesus seems to be asleep in the stern. Of course this frightens us, and so we try to shake Jesus awake, praying "Help, help!" During especially terrifying moments we may find ourselves saying what the disciples said: "Teacher, do you not care that we are perishing?" (Mark 4:38).

Heat-Moon's expedition took months. A journey with an illness can take decades or a lifetime. We must be involved in it or we'll capsize. But as with any trip, we're never in full control because there always will be storms that are more powerful than we are. To deal with them, we can invite Jesus to be our copilot. Heat-Moon needed a copilot. So do we.

5. "We know that all things work together for good for those who love God, who are called according to his purpose" (Rom 8:28). Scripture offers consolation, hope, challenges, and insights when we wrestle with an illness. For me, the Bible has been a source of emotional and spiritual life. This passage from Romans is one of my favorites because it helps me look for ways God has turned the bad of my pain into something good. Thanking God for those things gives me gratitude that my pain has not been wasted. God has brought good out of my suffering, even though that good has not yet included the complete physical healing I want.

6. "As long as you keep pointing to the specifics, you will miss the full meaning of your pain" (Henri Nouwen).[4] Father Nouwen wrote these words for himself during a time of profound darkness. Months earlier his eyes had turned inward and he had seen "a bottomless abyss" of his own nothingness. The above statement came as he neared the end of six months of recovery. He went on to note what would happen if he kept focusing on the specifics of his own particular illness:

> You will deceive yourself into believing that if people, circumstances, and events had been different, your pain would not exist. This may be partly true, but the deeper truth is that...your pain is the concrete way in which you participate in the pain of humanity.[5]

"The pain of humanity"—who wants to take part in that? And yet sooner or later, willingly or unwillingly, each of us does. That's what Jesus did, and so do we. The challenge is to participate without getting swallowed up by self-pity or bitterness or other destructive emotions.

My health has improved over time, but in one area I still can't do what most people can do. When I'm especially aware of this, a longing arises within me. That's not a problem—longing is part of the pain of humanity. But it's easy to move from longing into an internal whining that sucks happiness down into a poor-me whirlpool of misery. Over time, I've learned to deal with this by turning my eyes outward toward the suffering of others. In doing so, I find healing for them and for myself:

> Paradoxically, healing means moving from your pain to the pain. Jesus' suffering, concrete as it was, was the suffering of all humanity....Every time you can shift your attention, your suffering becomes easier to bear. It becomes a "light burden" and an "easy yoke" (Mt 11:30). Your very personal pain begins to be converted into *the* pain and you find new strength to live it. Herein lies the hope of all Christians."[6]

Conclusion

When I lose perspective on my illness, it helps me recall what my husband said after I told him about my split-picture prayer experience. "Can you believe I chose the rocky path?" I asked. "Of course," he said. "You'd be nuts not to choose it. Where does the rose-garden path lead?" I didn't know. "Where does the path with Jesus go?" That was easy: to heaven.

If we join Jesus on the rocky path of suffering and healing, we get no guarantees except his presence and his promise that he is leading us to fullness of life. We can cooperate by staying grounded in the reality of today, doing what we can do rather than being stopped by what we can't do. Using resources for support, we can remain open to kinds of healing that will bring us greater wholeness than we originally sought or imagined possible. And we can stay in touch with the fact that in this life, every person's path is a rocky one. Rose gardens only exist in yards and parks.

For You

Reflect on a serious illness from which you or a loved one suffer.

1. What is this illness? How has it impacted your life?
2. What are some of the positive ways you have dealt with it?
3. Over the next several days or weeks, I invite you to reflect on, and perhaps journal about, the quotes in this chapter. How might they help you in your situation?
   a. "Yesterday is gone. Tomorrow has not yet come. We have only today. Let us begin."
   b. "Only grief permits newness."
   c. "Keep returning to those to whom you belong and who keep you in the light."
   d. "Proceed as the way opens."
   e. "We know that all things work together for good for those who love God, who are called according to his purpose" (Rom 8:28).
   f. "As long as you keep pointing to the specifics, you will miss the full meaning of your pain."
4. Finally, a scripture:

We are afflicted in every way, but not crushed; perplexed, but not driven to despair; persecuted, but not forsaken; struck down, but not destroyed; always carrying in the body the death of Jesus, so that the life of Jesus may also be made visible in our bodies. (2 Cor 4:8–10)

CHAPTER 20

From Good Friday to Pentecost and Beyond

"For I know the plans I have for you," declares the Lord, "plans to prosper you and not to harm you, plans to give you hope and a future." (Jer 29:11 NIV)

People attending a healing Mass in Seattle saw something remarkable: A woman suffering from chronic bone pain was healed during the course of the Mass. Barbara arrived stiff and sore; she left pain-free. She says that during the Mass, "the pain I was so used to having slowly began to leave my body. The "getting old" morning stiffness was gone as well. The Lord did a miraculous healing of my body and a healing of my spirit as well!"[1]

If Barbara's entire healing had occurred within that one-hour Mass, we could expect the same for ourselves. All we'd have to do is find the right healer, the right prayer, the perfect pill, the quick-answer book. A story like Barbara's can tempt us to launch into a search for "The Healing."

In reality, what appeared to be an instant phenomenon for Barbara was the culmination of a two-year process that included daily prayer, the support of others, and forgiveness of people who had wounded her. Barbara's initial goal had been pain relief. What God gave her was fullness of life. Her physical cure took place suddenly but not isolated from other healings. What happened during Mass was a milestone in a journey.

Our own journey with God resembles Jesus' passage from Good Friday to Pentecost and beyond. His entire passover from death to full life is called the Paschal Mystery: Good Friday, Easter, the time period between the Resurrection and the Ascension, then the Ascension itself and finally, the sending of the Holy Spirit at Pentecost.

We live out the Paschal Mystery of Jesus Christ in our lives over and over in paschal cycles. Each cycle resembles what the disciples went through. Each is a process of healing, from death to new life, from Good Friday to Pentecost and beyond.[2]

The Paschal Cycle

John 12:24 portrays the paschal cycle this way: "Unless a grain of wheat falls to the earth and dies, it remains just a single grain; but if it dies, it bears much fruit." To me, this image has a poetic loveliness: A grain of wheat floats to the ground, settles into the soil, becomes transformed, arises to new, exuberant life. Ah, the beauty of it all—until it is we who are the grain, who fall down, lie buried in dirt, get rained on, and die in some way before arising to new life. When we undergo John 12:24 in our own lives, "poetic" rarely describes the experience. "Suffering" sounds more accurate.

As each year has different seasons, so does a paschal cycle: seasons that lead to transformation and abundant life. Just as our life up until now has already consisted of many years, our spiritual journey has already included many paschal cycles: many small and large journeys from Good Friday to Pentecost. What follows are the paschal cycle's five steps from the disciples' perspective and from ours. This is our pilgrimage of healing.

Step 1: Good Friday

Good Friday did not kill the disciples. Nevertheless Jesus' death spelled a type of death for them as well: the end of the life they had been living for three years. Most dying feels this way. Something occurs that we don't want, but it happens anyway. We may play a role in causing it, such as getting fired from a job. Often, however, something entirely outside our control comes along and shatters our heart.

Every story in this book includes Good Friday—a loss that is a type of death. Some losses are sudden—for example, Bud Welch losing his daughter in the Oklahoma City bombing—and some are gradual. For instance, chapter 11 tells of Mandy fleeing from her home when her husband threatened her with a gun. That was sudden, but the death of the marriage had actually begun years earlier and had grown like a cancer.

There are as many examples of Good Friday as there are transitions and losses in our lives. With each loss, some kind of death occurs. Something is over, and although it feels like the end, it actually isn't. It's a paschal death—a passover where one kind of life ends but, at the same time, a new life opens before us.

Unfortunately, a single event usually causes more than one paschal death. These are tangled like snarls in a fine gold chain. For instance, the collapse of Mandy's marriage also meant the loss of finances, a home, and dreams for marital happiness. One event, many losses. It took much work and much time to unravel the losses so that each could be healed.

Step 2: The Resurrection

After Good Friday comes Easter, an experience of life that differs from the past. The contrast may be great and usually is painful. This is not an Easter of chocolate, lilies, and bunnies. Instead, it's a change that resembles what the disciples underwent.

At the first Easter, the disciples were given a life that differed from what they had prior to Good Friday. They didn't ask for resurrection and a transformed savior. They probably would have preferred a return to the old ways of traveling with Jesus, eating with him, learning from him, and turning to him when disputes arose. Similarly, when we experience a life that differs from the past, we may not like what we have been given, but there it is anyway. It's common to yearn for a return to what existed before Good Friday. We want a resuscitation like Lazarus's, not a resurrection like Jesus'.

For example, a man named Craig had been married to Anita for a year. She worked on the ninetieth floor of a World Trade Center tower and was there when terrorists struck. Craig received a frantic call from his wife—then nothing. Hope evaporated when her body was found a week later. Naturally, Craig was devastated. Anita's physical death caused his paschal death. From life as a married man, he now entered into life as a widower.

When we are in this sort of pain, it may feel as though our new life is so disastrous that at best, we are mere survivors. God offers us resurrected, not resuscitated, life. God invites us to move forward because we cannot move backward. To do this—to accept our new life and fully live it—we must go through the next phase of the paschal cycle, the part called "forty days."

Step 3: The Forty Days

Acts 1:3 says the time between the Resurrection and the Ascension lasted forty days. In scripture, the number forty represents the time it takes to learn and be formed. For the disciples it was the time they spent learning and adjusting to their life without Jesus' bodily presence so they could be ready for the Ascension and Pentecost.

The forty-day phase is when most deep healing occurs. It's the time-consuming part of the paschal cycle where we grieve what we have lost and adjust to our new reality until we are ready for a new spirit that will empower us to live our new life. This phase requires our cooperation and active participation. We can resist it and remain stuck. Or we can cooperate.

Our grief can take many forms, including denial, anger, bargaining, and/or depression.

Denial. A huge loss such as Craig's usually includes an initial time of numbness and disbelief. I see this as God's gift of novocaine that carries us through the immediate crisis. Eventually, however, novocaine wears off and then it's time to deal with the pain. To refuse to do that is to follow in the footsteps of Joe (chapter 19), who left the "house" of his reality and waited for Jesus in a model home. Staying in denial sentences us to an on-going Good Friday where our wound remains open and agonizing.

Anger almost always surfaces as we deal with a paschal death. If our previous image of God has been destroyed by our Good Friday experience, it's likely that we'll be angry with God. A snugly, protective Jesus will seem neither snugly nor protective after a major loss.

One common form anger takes is "why": "Why did this happen?" "If God is all-loving and all-powerful, why doesn't he heal me?" "Why does God allow suffering in the world?" Healing rarely occurs through "why" questions because the mystery of God and human suffering goes beyond logic. Nevertheless, during the forty-day part of the paschal cycle the question "why?" naturally arises.

In *Prayers for Care Givers,* Patti Normile expresses the "why" of anger, plus a way to move beyond it.

Why?

Why? Why? Why?
Why must things be as they are?
Give me a new question, Lord.
I see there is no answer to my angry why?
Give me a *what:* What actions shall I take?
   What can I do to move on with life?
Give me a *who:* Who has gone this way before?
   Who can help me see my way?
Give me a *how:* How can I take care of just today?
   How can I turn my attitude around?
Thank you for the new questions, Lord.
   I'll work with them instead of asking why.[3]

Bargaining and *depression* are also common during the forty-day phase of the paschal cycle. Mandy knows those parts of grief. Long before the gun incident, she agonized over how she could save her marriage. Maybe if she was super-careful, her husband wouldn't get mad any more. Maybe if she prayed harder, Ben would be healed. Maybe if she could talk him into getting some counseling....The "maybe ifs" vanished on the night Mandy fled from her home, not even stopping for shoes or purse. Now came depression as the bleakness of her situation lay before her. All options had failed. No energy remained. All Mandy could do was weep.

None of the above phases of grief progress in order. And because the human spirit is not a linear object, we usually need to cycle back and forth through grief's phases. Eventually, however, we reach the *acceptance* phase (described in the paschal cycle's next step). How long does it take to get there? It depends on the severity of the wound, the depth of the need, the degree of our courage, and the amount of support we receive from others. The forty-day phase of the paschal cycle usually takes more than forty actual days. It's important to allow the right amount of time.

It's possible to extend this period for too long a time by getting locked into life before Good Friday. If so, we may become embittered or clinically depressed. However, the opposite also is true. We may try to go through the forty days too quickly. We, or others, can rush it. This is especially true with issues of forgiveness. It also is true with devastating losses, such as the death of a spouse. The pain can be so great that it feels unbearable. So of course we want it to be over. Common expressions are, "Why am I still in so much pain?" or "How long will I hurt this much?"

It would be nice to be able to say, "six months, then you're done," but no pat answers exist when we are immersed in suffering. "Forty days" may be two years; it may be less; it may be more. The important thing is to keep praying, keep reaching out for help, keep journeying with God. Actions can help. They can give us hope that, in turn, enhances healing.

Step 4: The Ascension

This is the acceptance phase of the grieving process, where we let go of the old. As with the forty-day phase, we can actively participate in it or we can resist.

It's natural to want to hang onto the past like Mary Magdalene clung to Jesus after his resurrection (John 20:17). Letting go is painful. Furthermore, release is impossible until closure with the old takes place, that is, until we have completed the forty-day part of the paschal cycle. If it isn't occurring—if we cannot seem to let go—it may be because we have not yet completed the forty-day period.

When we do let go, we release the past to God. Sometimes it's painful to release something because we want it back. That's

Craig's situation. He longs for the marriage he had before September 11. After he's gone through the forty-day period of the paschal cycle, Ascension will enable him to experience the blessing of the time he had with his wife.

Sometimes, however, it's painful to let go of a traumatic event that strangled our past and continues to harm our present. That was Mandy's situation. For her, letting go meant releasing her pain and her ex-husband to God. She let go so that God could deal with Ben and so that she could be freed from the past.

Unlike Jesus' ascension, we may need to let go again and again, each time releasing our loss a bit more. Rituals help and can come to mind if we allow our imagination to run free. For instance, a year after Mandy's divorce, she attended a live performance of the music she had listened to on tape for months: Vivaldi's "Four Seasons" symphony. "It was the first concert I ever attended by myself," she says. "I looked back on the last four seasons of my life and saw how much better my life had become. Something about that concert, going alone, and the fact that it came exactly four seasons after I was introduced to the music, made me believe I could go forward into future seasons of my life, mostly healed from the hurts of my past."

Letting go neither denies the depth of our wound nor trivializes our loss. Rather, it lets our loss rise to heaven, as Jesus ascended after Easter. This frees us to enter into the final phase of the paschal cycle: Pentecost.

Step 5: Pentecost

According to Acts 2, Pentecost was when the disciples received a new spirit for the new life they already were living. Before the coming of the Holy Spirit, they were hiding behind locked doors. They had a new life but lacked the power to live it.

In the Pentecost phase, God gives us a new spirit for our new life. We cannot seize it or generate it ourselves, regardless of how much we want to do so. Like the original Pentecost of two thousand years ago, the Holy Spirit we received at our baptism was pure gift. Now, we receive a greater fullness of God's Spirit, an increased power to be who God created us to be.

When we have been wounded and are journeying through a paschal cycle, the Holy Spirit cannot bless us in a new way for our new life until we have gone through Good Friday, Easter, "forty days," and the Ascension. There is no shortcut to Pentecost.

What does the Pentecost phase of the paschal cycle feel like? For me,

- It feels totally real, like being truly present in this moment.

- It feels as though, at last, I am able to be myself.

- It feels as though some inner turmoil has finally been calmed, perhaps like the Sea of Galilee after Jesus calmed the storm. Even in the midst of external turmoil, there is inner peace.

- It feels as though I now have the gift of courage to live the life God created me to live.

- It feels like empowerment, not to muscle through a situation, and not to "pay back" someone who hurt me, but rather empowerment to reach out to others in healing, loving ways.

Two Cautions

It's good to keep two cautions in mind as regards the paschal cycle because it can be either destructive or life-giving. First, the journey from Good Friday to Pentecost wasn't a solo for the disciples and shouldn't be a solo for us. Naively believing we can do it alone puts us in harm's way. Like entering the ocean for a swim, we need at least one "buddy":

> When we stare life's chaos fully in the face, someone or something had better be holding us or that darkness will destroy us rather than make us stronger....It is said that whatever doesn't kill you makes you stronger. True, though sometimes things will kill you, if you face them alone."[4]

A second caution: To avoid discouragement and disillusionment, we need realistic expectations. What we can expect with a significant wound is that it will require more than one journey through the paschal cycle. Whenever we look into the face of an old wound and a new paschal cycle, it may feel like, "Oh no, *this* wound *again*. I thought I was healed of that." We were. We were healed at a level that freed us to live more fully at that particular stage of our life. Now, however, God invites us to deeper healing. We can say yes or no to that invitation. When we say yes, the result is more freedom, more courage, more empowerment, more abundant life.

The journey we take through the life of Christ every year in the church's liturgy can be our own journey—our own paschal cycle—that brings an increase in abundant life each time we go through it. God continually invites us to deeper healing so we can have greater fullness of life. Day-by-day, year-by-year, God wants us to experience the truth of Revelation 21:5: "See, I am making all things new."

For You

Paul said, "I forget what is behind me and do my best to reach what is ahead" (Phil 3:13 GNT). A paschal death can never truly be forgotten, but it can be transformed. Think of where you've been and where you are now. Where is your life being transformed? Consider past and present losses, then reflect on the five steps in the paschal cycle as it relates to the losses.

1. *Good Friday.* What kind of Good Fridays have you experienced? What kind of losses have you suffered because of them? For example, loss of physical ability, loss of career, loss of a dream, loss of relationship(s) through death or estrangement. The depth of your pain will be especially great if Good Friday caused many losses.

2. *Resurrection.* What "new life" do you currently have in the aftermath of your Good Fridays? In other words, what have been the consequences of the paschal death(s) you have suffered?

3. *The forty days.* This is the confusing, time-consuming, hard-work phase.
   a. How far have you progressed in it in the past?
   b. What sort of forty-day period are you going through now?
   c. In what ways have you experienced grief as a result of your loss(es), for example, denial, anger, bargaining, depression? Have any of these abated somewhat?

4. *Ascension.*
   a. What forty-day phase have you already experienced to the point where you could let go of your pain and release it to God?
   b. What pain do you now feel invited to release?
   c. If an all-at-once release is impossible, can you begin to hand some aspect of your loss(es) over to God? Can you hand it over for a brief moment? Momentary

release can lead to greater and greater release over a period of days/weeks/months.

5. *Pentecost.* Wherever you have progressed through the first four steps of the paschal cycle, this is a good time to ask God to send you the peace and love of the Holy Spirit. Spend some time in prayer and openness and expect God's gift to come to you in the upcoming days/weeks/months. A gift cannot be compelled; it can only be received. Pray for the grace to receive that gift.

6. Finally, a prayer:

Lord Jesus Christ, you who went through the ultimate paschal cycle during your time on earth, be with me as I go through mine. Lead me, Lord, and I will follow. God of all creation, thank you that in the midst of my journey you are making all things new. Spirit of the Living God, thank you for your gifts of strength, love, and healing. Amen.

Looking Ahead

When we experience healing, we want it to last and continue to grow. How can that happen? One of the best ways is through reaching out to others. "Give, and it will be given to you," said Jesus. "A good measure, pressed down, shaken together, running over, will be put into your lap" (Luke 6:38a). The final chapter in this book looks at how to pass our healing on to others, and why this can be life-giving for us.

CHAPTER 21

Passing on Our Healing to Others

God helps us in all our troubles so that we are able to
help others who have all kinds of troubles, using the
same help that we ourselves have received from God.
(2 Cor 1:4 GNT)

In January 1994 my husband and I traveled to Death Valley
during a week when other tourists were delightfully scarce.
Aside from park employees, we had the place to ourselves. We
saw a land of sunshine and silence, of sunrises and sunsets, and
astonishing beauty. And we saw Badwater, which, at 280 feet
below sea level, is a brackish pool surrounded by miles of salt
deposits. Some deposits are over 1,000 feet thick. What we
didn't see at Badwater was very much life. Why is this?

If I had been asked that question before our visit, I would
have said the lack of life came from a lack of water. In fact,
water roars into the area when it rains hard. But because
Badwater is the lowest point in the Western Hemisphere, water
cannot flow to lower terrain. Instead, it stays until it evapo-
rates, leaving more and more salt and less and less life.

When we are ill, we may be incapable of offering much to
others because our illness has left us in a personal Death Valley.
As we become healed, however, the blessing of what we've

received needs to start flowing outward: "Let the one who believes in me drink," said Jesus. Then, "out of the believer's heart shall flow rivers of living water." (John 7:38)

The alternative to reaching out to others is to focus solely on our own healing and concerns. But if we do that, the living water we've received will turn briny. New life will gradually evaporate and leave us wondering what happened to the healing and the spiritual experiences we once had.

To keep what we've been given, we need to pass it on to others. That is what this chapter covers: How to pass on our healing to others and receive additional healing for ourselves.

Ways to Be a Blessing to Others

Doug works in an auto repair shop where every day he makes a point of affirming his coworkers in some small way, telling each of them something good he sees in the work they're doing or in who they are.

Alice belongs to a church group that hosts receptions after funerals. She brings a salad or cookies to receptions and helps serve the food.

Doug and Alice are both a blessing to others, although few people would call Doug's work "holy" or "ministry" because it doesn't take place at church. Actually, any time we reach out to others with love, we are bringing God to a world that desperately needs healing. People whose lives we can touch include family, friends and neighbors, the poor, people at work, the faith community, and those we encounter in unexpected moments.

Family

As I was feeding my newborn twins at 2:00 A.M. one night, red-eyed and weeping from exhaustion, words from scripture came to mind: "I was hungry and you gave me food, I was thirsty and you gave me something to drink" (Matt 25:35). Jesus says whatever we do for "the least of our brothers," we do for him. He places no limits on who they might be. An act of love to anyone—including family members—is ministry to Jesus.

Friends and Neighbors

When Liz (chapter 20) was diagnosed with cancer, friends and neighbors reached out to her in dozens of imaginative ways: They brought food; they created a fund to pay for a house cleaner; they sent cards of encouragement; they prayed; they gave hugs; they asked how she was doing; they took her to chemotherapy treatments; they invited her children over to play and gave them rides to sports practices. Liz says thoughtfulness like this made a huge difference to her and the family. In the same way that Simon of Cyrene helped Jesus carry his cross on Calvary, friends and neighbors helped Liz and her family carry the cross of an illness.

The Poor

Madison and her three children moved into subsidized housing in our neighborhood, then encountered a problem: Most of their income was needed for rent and utilities, leaving little or nothing for food, clothing, and furnishings. What could be done? Relief came from the St. Vincent de Paul Society in our parish. Two members visited Madison in her home and worked with her to meet the family's most pressing needs. Help included finding and delivering used beds and a kitchen table. It also included showing Madison how to use food stamps, where to find a food bank, and how to access public transportation in our area. Within three months the family was settled in and functioning.

Caring for the poor may be local, as in the work of a St. Vincent de Paul Society. Or it may extend far from home through donations of money or time to groups such as Habitat for Humanity or Doctors Without Borders. Whatever we do in this area, we are the hands and heart of Christ to those for whom God has a special concern. "Give justice to the weak and the orphan; maintain the right of the lowly and the destitute," says Psalm 82:3. We live those words whenever we reach out to the poor.

People at Work

In the Gospels a gap exists between Jesus' birth in Bethlehem and the start of his public ministry thirty years later. It's as if he was unemployed for decades then finally landed a job as Savior of the world.

Actually, Jesus was rejected by people in Nazareth in part because they saw him as their carpenter, not their Messiah. But surely he must have brought the same love into his carpentry career that he later showed in public ministry. I imagine he did what Doug does at the auto repair shop: affirms people for who they are and what they do, shows patience, cares about the work environment and the quality of the job being done, includes everyone, excludes no one. In a job setting, even one Christ-like person will have a healing effect on the entire workforce.

The Faith Community

Jesus went about all the cities and villages, teaching in their synagogues, and proclaiming the good news of the kingdom, and curing every disease and every sickness. When he saw the crowds, he had compassion for them, because they were harassed and helpless, like sheep without a shepherd. Then he said to his disciples, "The harvest is plentiful, but the laborers are few; therefore ask the Lord of the harvest to send out laborers into his harvest." (Matt 9:35–38)

For two thousand years Christians have heard this passage as a personal call to do something for those who are "harassed and helpless," in need of teaching, healing, and all sorts of other care. Often that care occurs in and through a church. Some hear God calling them to ordained ministry or a lay ministry career. Most people simply hear a call to offer a bit of time and talent to their faith community. It might mean singing in the choir, teaching Sunday school, being an usher, collecting donations for a food bank, offering prayer ministry, or any of a hundred other options. When it comes to being a healing influence within and through the church, God calls for many yeses because the need is still great but the laborers are few.

People We Encounter in Unexpected Moments

As my daughter and I waited in a purchasing line one day, we noticed that the woman ahead of us was close to tears. She wanted to return an item but only spoke Spanish while the salesperson only spoke English. My daughter knows Spanish, so she approached the woman and offered to translate for her. Five minutes later the item had been returned and everyone was smiling.

Good Samaritan deeds tell people they are not alone. What seems small to us may mean a lot to someone in momentary crisis. All we need is alertness and a willingness to occasionally go out of our way for a person whose need lies outside of our planned day. Even a smile can be healing for someone who is upset or in grief or simply having a bad day.

Discerning God's Call

To serve God effectively without destroying ourselves, we need the gift of discernment; the opposite leads to futility and frustration. The following story from Luke, which occurred at the home of Simon Peter's mother-in-law, gives us an idea of the importance of discernment in Jesus' ministry:

> As the sun was setting, all those who had any who were sick with various kinds of diseases brought them to him; and he laid his hands on each of them and cured them....At daybreak he departed and went into a deserted place. And the crowds were looking for him; and when they reached him, they wanted to prevent him from leaving them. But he said to them, "I must proclaim the good news of the kingdom of God to the other cities also; for I was sent for this purpose." (Luke 4:40–43)

Healing was part of "the good news of the kingdom of God" that Jesus proclaimed, and he is our role model for discerning where, when, who, how, and what that means for us today. How is God calling us to pass on our healing to others? Where is he calling us to serve? How much or how little does he want us to do? There are no automatic answers to these questions.

If I had been Jesus in the above situation, I probably would have gone with the crowd, continued ministering to them, missed the rest of God's call, and worked until I was too exhausted to move. That's because when I see a need, I tend to assume I'm the one who should meet it—now. It's taken me years to learn that that's not discernment. That's going ahead of God. Then comes trouble:

- When I go ahead of God, my work lacks the results I hope for because it lacks God's power.

- When I do what God isn't calling me to do, I have less time—or no time—for what God does want me to do. In the above scripture, Jesus' return to town would have meant a lack of ministry to people in other areas. He would have been a local sensation but little else.

- When I do what God is calling me to do plus what he isn't calling me to do, I burn out and get resentful. Often my health suffers as well.

- When I do what someone else is meant to do, I deprive that person of an opportunity to serve God.

- When I resist doing something I'm called to do, such as move to a different parish and serve there (chapter 15), my spiritual life dries up and my happiness level sinks.

So how can we discern where God is calling us? Whole books and entire careers are devoted to answering that question. But briefly, I have learned to pay attention to personal prayer, scripture, my faith community, and circumstances.

Personal Prayer

If Jesus hadn't gone "to a lonely place" after the previous day's incredible events, he might not have realized he was meant to continue his ministry in other towns. For me, a process of discernment starts by sitting down with God and getting into prayerful listening and thinking.

Scripture

Scripture helps us avoid mistakes because God will never ask us to do something that goes against his Word. But scripture also can apply to us very personally. For instance, two separate events in one week gave me a sense that God was calling me to move to another parish: First came a prayer experience. Then came that Sunday's gospel: "...If any want to become my followers, let them deny themselves and take up their cross and follow me" (Mark 8:34). The reading confirmed my earlier prayer experience, and although I didn't like the message, I knew what it meant for me.

Faith Community

"Now we see in a mirror, dimly," Paul said (1 Cor 13:12a). In other words, in this life our sense of God is, at best, a little foggy. That's why we need the Body of Christ as a safety net. For example, Erin was getting a divorce and feeling so overwhelmed at the idea of single parenting that one day she told several of us she had decided to give her husband full custody of their four boys. "Wait!" we exclaimed in near unison. "Alex goes on binges and disappears for days at a time. He throws furniture. He beats you and the boys. Please don't give him custody of these children. It will destroy them." We also told Erin we would support her in her role as a single parent. By the end of the conversation she saw the craziness of her initial idea and felt that, with help, she could parent her children without a husband, and so she did. It was often hard and sometimes painful, but the family survived and even thrived.

Circumstances

When Erin was finding a part-time job, getting a divorce, and adjusting to single parenting, she knew that all her time and energy needed to be devoted to those tasks. But as things settled down, she decided that once a month she could volunteer for a few hours at a food bank. Her work helped the customers and also gave Erin a perspective on her own life and its many blessings.

Because circumstances do not stay locked in place, God's call to us this year may not be the same for the next. That's why I personally take the month of August and spend a few minutes each day looking at my current circumstances and prayerfully discerning where I sense I'm being called to reach out to others. By the end of the month I usually have a sense of what commitments I will make for the upcoming school year.

Benefits of Reaching Out to Others

When we give of ourselves to others, obviously they benefit. What's less obvious is that we too benefit. This can surprise us even though Jesus told his followers it would happen: "Give, and it will be given to you. A good measure, pressed down, shaken together, running over, will be put into your lap" (Luke 6:38).

What kind of healing might we experience when we reach out to others? Here are a few examples.

Physical Healing

An on-the-job injury to Neal's left arm had put him on permanent disability. The arm's circulation was so poor that it was weak, cold, and lacking a detectable pulse. This problem persisted for thirteen years until Neal decided to join a lay ministry training class.[1] One day as he was reading *Healing as a Parish Ministry* for an assignment, his arm began to feel warm. Puzzled, he thought he'd see if he could find a pulse. To his amazement, he found it easily. He says, "It was so unbelievable that it took a few weeks before I could accept the fact that God in his wonderful mercy had performed a miracle for me."

Miracles do happen when we reach out to others. Most are gradual; a few are instantaneous. It would be great if we could figure out exactly how they occur because then we could duplicate our actions, thoughts, and so on, and bring about similar results for other needs. But God cannot be boxed in like that. Perhaps openness during ministry (or in Neal's case, preparation for ministry) gives us an openness to receiving healing for ourselves. Or perhaps as we become a channel of God's healing to someone else, some of that grace stays with us. Theories abound but answers elude us. As always, we bow before the mystery of God's love and mercy.

Emotional Healing

Years of medical care, counseling, prayer, and participation in a support group had diminished some of the pain from the sexual abuse Chuck had experienced as a child. Nevertheless, he still suffered from flashbacks that left his nerves feeling bare and raw. At those moments he not only remembered the violence; he relived it.

An easing of flashbacks took place after Chuck began working with homeless teens, many of whom had left home as a way to escape from sexual abuse. Chuck's background gave him an ability to identify with their pain and reach out to them in nonintrusive ways. Getting to know the most wounded youths showed him how far he had come in his own healing. In especially brutal cases, kids' coping and inner strength showed Chuck that the human spirit can rise above even the most devastating traumas. "It gave me hope," he now says. And it also gave him a depth of emotional healing that had not occurred through other avenues.

Spiritual Healing

Valerie's husband was dying of cancer and she was mad at God. Why Jim? Why her? They'd been serving God for years, and now where was he when they needed him? Obviously God was like her alcoholic father: mute, not present in a crisis—in a word, untrustworthy.

Chapter 18 describes Valerie's struggles to forgive her father. Jim's illness brought to light a wound around the issue of trust. For a while, she was so angry that she shut herself off from God, only allowing herself to be open during the prayer ministry that she and two women offered to others. "In prayer ministry I could hear God," she says, "and that carried over into the rest of my life. I prayed with somebody and then shortly afterward I would experience God's love for me." These experiences helped Valerie through the final days of Jim's illness and the period of acute grief that followed. Over time, her distrust of God was replaced by an awakening to God's constant presence, regardless of Valerie's mood or circumstances. Her favorite Bible chapter became Romans 8:

> "We know that all things work together for good for those who love God, who are called according to his purpose....I am convinced that neither death, nor life, nor angels, nor rulers, nor things present, nor things to come, nor powers, nor height, nor depth, nor anything else in all creation, will be able to separate us from the love of God in Christ Jesus our Lord." (Rom 8:28, 38–39)

For You

1. "Great works do not always lie in our way," said St. Francis de Sales, "but every moment we may do little ones excellently, that is, with great love."[2] Looking at your current life and the people whose lives you touch, where have you been offering loving deeds to others? Consider the following people:

   Family (including your extended family)

   Friends and neighbors

The poor
People at work
The faith community
People you encounter in unexpected moments

2. In reaching out to these people, have you found any of your experiences to be a blessing for you? If so, in what ways?

3. Now I invite you to look again at these groups, and prayerfully discern where God may be calling you to increase your love for them in a small yet tangible way. For instance:

- If you have a neighbor who, like Liz, is being treated for cancer, are there any ideas you've drawn from this chapter that you could use in your neighbor's situation?

- Like Doug, you might pray for the grace to see coworkers or loved ones through God's eyes and begin affirming them for specific traits or behavior you've observed.

- If you haven't been active in your faith community, is there some area into which God may be calling you to serve? Even the smallest task is important.

- What ideas come to mind as regards serving the poor? Cleaning out your closets and donating usable items to a thrift store? Donating to a food bank? Joining a service group in your faith community? Again, every act is ministry to Jesus.

4. Finally, we need grace in order to have the strength to do God's holy work. We need to be people of prayer. Pray your own spontaneous prayers. Pray alone. Pray with others. Pray the psalms. Pray with words of the saints,

such as Francis of Assisi ("Lord, make me an instrument of your peace"). Here's an ancient prayer I love. To me it expresses my desire for God's fullness in my life—in who I am, in what I am doing, in where I am going, and in how I am being healed:

God be in my head and in my understanding.
God be in my eyes and in my looking.
God be in my mouth and in my speaking.
God be in my heart and in my thinking.
God be at my end and in my departing.

Notes

Introduction

1. Leo Thomas, O.P., and Jan Alkire, *Healing as a Parish Ministry*, 2nd ed. (Seattle: Byron Books, 2000), 138.

Chapter 1

1. Kinds of wounds are described in *Healing Ministry: A Practical Guide* by Leo Thomas, O.P., with Jan Alkire (Kansas City, Mo.: Sheed & Ward, 1994). Chapter 6 gives an overview of the topic. Chapters 7 through 11 cover healing of those wounds. Reflection questions at the end of each chapter are useful for personal healing.

2. David's story is described in detail in *Healing as a Parish Ministry*, chapter 2, "What is Health?"

3. Lewis B. Smedes, *The Art of Forgiving* (New York: Ballantine Books, 1997), xi.

4. St. Augustine, *Confessions,* trans. R. S. Pine-Coffin (London: Penguin Books, Ltd., 1961), 164.

Chapter 4

1. Larry Dossey, M.D., *Healing Words: The Power of Prayer and the Practice of Medicine* (New York: Harper Collins, 1993).

2. *Catechism of the Catholic Church (CCC)* (Washington, D.C.: U.S. Catholic Conference, 1994), ¶2560.

Chapter 5

1. This material about praise comes from a worship teaching in the Institute for Christian Ministries' Formation for Healing Ministry program. Information about FHM can be found at www.healingministry.org.

2. Praying in tongues ("glossolalia") is one of the gifts of the Holy Spirit that the disciples received at the first Pentecost. In *Healing Ministry: A Practical Guide,* Father Thomas wrote, "Of all the gifts of the Spirit that exist, glossolalia has caused more disturbances—literally and figuratively—than any of the others." To learn more about this misunderstood gift, see pages 212–13 in the above book.

Chapter 6

1. Father Henry Fehren, "Confession, Anyone?" *U.S. Catholic* (October 1989): 40.

Chapter 7

1. *Healing Words,* chapter 5, "How to Pray and What to Pray For."

Chapter 8

1. *Healing Ministry: A Practical Guide,* 219.

2. Other styles of scripture meditation include: Benedictine (featuring *Lectio Divina* and going back to the fourth and fifth centuries), Franciscan (from the thirteenth century's St. Francis of Assisi), and Thomistic (the method of prayer recommended by St. Thomas Aquinas). For clear descriptions and practicum options for each of these meditation styles, I recommend *Prayer and Temperament* by Chester P. Michael and Marie C. Norrisey (Charlottesville, Va.: The Open Door, 1991).

3. *Confessions,* 177–78.

Chapter 9

1. *Confessions,* 231.

2. Dennis Linn, Sheila Fabricant Linn, and Matthew Linn, *Don't Forgive Too Soon* (Mahwah, N.J.: Paulist Press), 1997.

3. Ibid., 61.

4. "Write It Down, Feel Better," *Remedy* (July/August 1999): 10.

Chapter 10

1. What I call contemplative prayer, others sometimes call by different names, such as "prayer of quiet" or "centering prayer." Distinctions exist between them but are beyond the scope of this book. Here, I call prayer that is beyond words, images, and thoughts "contemplative prayer." For more on this topic, I recommend *Open Mind, Open Heart* by Father Thomas Keating (Warwick, N.Y.: Amity House, 1986).

2. Father Edward Hays, "An Invitation to Prayer," *Catholic Update* (February 1992).

3. Ibid.

Chapter 11

1. Richard Rohr, O.F.M., "Religion, Spirituality and Pain: Seeking an Icon of Transformation," *The Journal of Christian Healing,* 22, nos. 1 & 2 (spring/summer, 2000): 65.

2. Melanie Bowden, "Praying on Foot," *Catholic Digest* (December 2001): 13.

3. Rohr, "Religion, Spirituality and Pain," 64.

Chapter 12

1. *Prayer and Temperament*, 8.

2. Ibid., 21.

3. Kathleen Norris, *Amazing Grace* (New York: Riverhead Books, 1998), 61.

Chapter 13

1. William Ernest Henley, *Echoes (1888). No. 4. In Memoriam R. T. Hamilton Bruce ("Invictus"), st. 4*, quoted in *Bartlett's Familiar Quotations, 15th edition* (Boston: Little, Brown & Co., 1980), 663.

2. St. Aelred of Rievaulx, *Christian Friendship*, quoted in *The Harper Religious and Inspirational Quotation Companion* (New York: Harper & Row, 1989), 191.

3. "Companions for the Spiritual Journey" has been a program offered by the Institute for Christian Ministries.

Chapter 14

1. Chapters 4 and 5 in *Healing Ministry: A Practical Guide* address the topic of listening. Chapter 5 describes four qualities of a good listener (self-sacrifice, respect, unconditional love, serenity), plus various kinds of helpful responses that good listeners can offer.

2. M. Scott Peck, M.D., *The Road Less Traveled* (New York: Simon & Schuster, 1978), 133.

Chapter 15

1. Mark Francis, C.S.V., "Have Sacraments Changed?" *Catholic Update* (September 1997).

2. Given the variety of words and beliefs that Christian churches have for worship services, it is difficult to address this

topic without excluding either some people or some important tenets of faith. I write as a Catholic Christian who believes in, and honors, the Real Presence of Christ in the Eucharist (i.e., the Mass). However, to help the greatest number of readers understand the healing power of community worship, in this chapter I take an ecumenical approach to Sunday services.

3. Robert A. Hummer et al., "Religious Involvement and U.S. Adult Mortality," *Demography* 36, no. 2 (May 1999): 273.

4. Cardinal Joseph Bernardin, "The Eucharist and Healing," *Eucharistic Minister*, no. 138 (September 1995): 1–2.

5. Tom McGrath, "Do What in Remembrance of Whom?" *U.S. Catholic* (July 1994): 9.

Chapter 16

1. Barbara Leahy Shlemon, *Healing Prayer* (Notre Dame: Ave Maria Press, 1976), 16.

2. Morton Kelsey, *Healing and Christianity* (Minneapolis, Minn.: Augsburg, 1995), 42.

3. For some Christians, such as Roman Catholics and Episcopalians, anointing of the sick is one of their seven sacraments. Others do not regard it as a sacrament. For the sake of including all readers, in this chapter I have chosen to write about anointing of the sick without reference to its sacramentality.

4. Joseph Martos, *The Church's Sacraments: Anointing of the Sick* (Liguori, Mo.: Liguori Publications, 1991), 14.

5. The Catholic Church has a specific ritual for the dying. Called *viaticum* (Latin: "on the way with you"), its goal is to help people prepare for their final journey to God. These last rites are not the same as the church's sacrament of anointing of the sick.

6. In the Catholic Church, the sacrament of anointing of the sick is always administered by a priest, using oil blessed by a

bishop. This should not be confused with informal anointing by lay people using oil blessed by a priest. The former rite is a sacrament, the latter is not.

Chapter 17

1. Jean Shepherd, *In God We Trust: All Others Pay Cash* (New York: Broadway Books/Random House, 2000), 119.

2. A number of Christian faiths now reach out to postabortion women and men just as the father of the prodigal son reached out to his wayward child. They embrace them in love and journey with them through healing of the deep hurt that abortion causes.

An international ministry called "Project Rachel" offers help in postabortion healing. It focuses on sacramental reconciliation through trained Catholic priests authorized by their bishop to engage in this ministry. For more information, phone the National Office of Post-Abortion Reconciliation and Healing toll-free at 800-5WE-CARE (800-593-2273). Also, a nondenominational Christian organization offers postabortion referrals for local ministry. Phone: 800-395-4357.

3. *Catechism of the Catholic Church,* ¶ 1864.

4. In the Catholic Church, what was once called confession is now called the sacrament of reconciliation, and what once occurred in a tiny confessional now takes place in a room specially set aside for receiving the sacrament either face-to-face or behind a screen. The choice is ours.

Communal celebrations of the sacrament have also become popular since the Vatican II Council. In whatever way the rite is celebrated, it's important to choose the priest carefully. We stand bare-souled when we confess our sins to someone else. That person needs to have a compassionate heart.

Chapter 18

1. Bud Welch, "Where Healing Begins," *Guideposts* (May 1999): 4.

2. Terry McGuire, "Execution Won't Bring My Daughter Back," *The Catholic Northwest Progress* (February 5, 1998): 9.

3. I am indebted to Lewis B. Smedes for his wisdom in the area of forgiveness. I have been helped personally by his books, *Forgive and Forget: Healing the Hurts We Don't Deserve* (San Francisco: Harper & Row, 1984), and *The Art of Forgiving* (cited earlier).

4. *The Art of Forgiving,* 93.

5. Welch, "Where Healing Begins," 5.

6. McGuire, "Execution Won't Bring My Daughter Back," 9.

7. Bishop George L. Thomas, from homily delivered on September 14, 2001, at St. James Cathedral, Seattle, during the National Day of Prayer and Remembrance. Quoted in *The Catholic Northwest Progress*, (September 20, 2001): 4.

Chapter 19

1. Anne Lamott, *Traveling Mercies: Some Thoughts on Faith* (New York: Anchor Books, 1999), 118–19.

2. Henri J. M. Nouwen, *The Inner Voice of Love: A Journey Through Anguish to Freedom* (New York: Doubleday, 1996), 46.

3. William Least Heat-Moon, *River Horse* (Boston: Houghton Mifflin, 1999), xii.

4. *The Inner Voice of Love,* 103.

5. Ibid., 103.

6. Ibid., 103–4.

Chapter 20

1. Barbara Fortin, "One Step at a Time," *Gleanings* (August/September 1999): 3.

2. The concepts of the paschal cycle come from a book by Father Ronald Rolheiser, O.M.I., entitled *The Holy Longing: A Search for Christian Spirituality* (New York: Doubleday, 1999). I am grateful to Father Rolheiser for his insights and wisdom.

3. Patti Normile, *Prayers for Care Givers* (Cincinnati, Ohio: St. Anthony Messenger Press, 1995), 66.

4. Ronald Rolheiser, O.M.I., "Facing Up to the Chaos," *The Catholic Northwest Progress* (January 13, 2000): 11.

Chapter 21

1. The training class Neal was taking at the time of his healing is called Formation for Healing Ministry. Offered by the Institute for Christian Ministries (ICM), the program is designed for use in one's own faith community. For more information, see ICM's website: www.healingministry.org.

2. St. Francis de Sales, *On the Love of God*, quoted in *The Harper Religious and Inspirational Quotation Companion*, 338.

Bibliography

Aelred of Rievaulx, St. *Christian Friendship*. Quoted in *The Harper Religious and Inspirational Quotation Companion*. New York: Harper & Row, 1989.

Augustine of Hippo, St. *Confessions*. Translated by R. S. Pine-Coffin. London: Penguin Books Ltd., 1961.

Bernardin, Cardinal Joseph. "The Eucharist and Healing." *Eucharistic Minister,* 138 (September 1995): 1–2.

Bowden, Melanie. "Praying on Foot." *Catholic Digest* (December 2001): 13.

Catechism of the Catholic Church. Washington D.C.: U.S. Catholic Conference, 1994.

DeSales, Francis. *On the Love of God*. Quoted in *The Harper Religious and Inspirational Quotation Companion*. New York: Harper & Row, 1989.

Dossey, Larry, M.D. *Healing Words: The Power of Prayer and the Practice of Medicine*. New York: Harper Collins, 1993.

Fehren, Father Henry. "Confession, Anyone?" *U.S. Catholic* (October 1989): 40.

Fortin, Barbara. "One Step at a Time." *Gleanings* (August/ September 1999): 3, 6.

Francis, Mark, C.S.V. "Have Sacraments Changed?" *Catholic Update* (September 1997).

Hays, Father Edward. "An Invitation to Prayer." *Catholic Update* (February 1992).

Heat-Moon, William Least. *River Horse.* Boston: Houghton Mifflin, 1999.

Hummer, Robert A. et al. "Religious Involvement and U.S. Adult Mortality." *Demography* 36, no. 2 (May 1999): 273–85.

Kelsey, Father Morton. *Healing and Christianity.* Minneapolis: Augsberg, 1995.

Lamott, Anne. *Traveling Mercies: Some Thoughts on Faith.* New York: Anchor Books, 1999.

Linn, Dennis, Sheila Fabricant Linn, and Matthew Linn. *Don't Forgive Too Soon.* Mahwah, N.J.: Paulist Press, 1997.

Martos, Joseph. *The Church's Sacraments: Anointing of the Sick.* Liguori, Mo.: Liguori Publications, 1991.

McGrath, Tom. "Do What in Remembrance of Whom?" *U.S. Catholic* (July 1994): 9.

McGuire, Terry. "Execution Won't Bring My Daughter Back." *The Catholic Northwest Progress,* 5 (February 1998): 9.

Michael, Monsignor Chester P., and Marie C. Norrisey. *Prayer and Temperament: Different Prayer Forms for Different Personality Types.* Charlottesville, Va.: The Open Door, 1991.

Normile, Patti. *Prayers for Care Givers.* Cincinnati, Ohio: St. Anthony Messenger Press, 1995.

Norris, Kathleen. *Amazing Grace.* New York: Riverhead Books, 1998.

Nouwen, Henri J. M. *The Inner Voice of Love: A Journey Through Anguish to Freedom.* New York: Doubleday, 1996.

Peck, M. Scott, M.D. *The Road Less Traveled.* New York: Simon & Schuster, 1978.

Rohr, Richard, O.F.M. "Religion, Spirituality and Pain: Seeking an Icon of Transformation." *The Journal of Christian Healing,* vol. 22, nos. 1 & 2 (spring/summer, 2000): 51–69.

Rolheiser, Ronald, O.M.I. "Facing Up to the Chaos." *The Catholic Northwest Progress* (January 13, 2000): 11.

Rolheiser, Ronald, O.M.I. *The Holy Longing: A Search for Christian Spirituality.* New York: Doubleday, 1999.

Shepherd, Jean. *In God We Trust: All Others Pay Cash.* New York: Broadway Books/Random House, 2000.

Shlemon, Barbara Leahy. *Healing Prayer.* Notre Dame, Ind.: Ave Maria Press, 1976.

Smedes, Lewis B. *The Art of Forgiving.* New York: Ballantine Books, 1997.

Thomas, Bishop George L. Homily delivered on September 14, 2001, at St. James Cathedral in Seattle during the National Day of Prayer and Remembrance. Quoted in *The Catholic Northwest Progress,* 20 (September 2001): 4.

Thomas, Leo, O.P., and Alkire, Jan. *Formation for Healing Ministry.* Seattle: Institute for Christian Ministries, 1997 (Year II) and 1998 (Year I).

Thomas, Leo, O.P., with Alkire Jan. *Healing Ministry: A Practical Guide.* Kansas City, Mo.: Sheed & Ward, 1994.

Thomas, Leo, O.P., and Alkire, Jan. *Healing as a Parish Ministry,* 2nd ed. Seattle: Byron Books, 2000. (First ed.: Ave Maria Press, 1992).

Welch, Bud. "Where Healing Begins." *Guideposts* (May 1999): 4.

"Write It Down, Feel Better," *Remedy,* July/August 1999, 10.

Further Reading

The following have been helpful to me for healing and for spiritual growth. Many are cited in this book.

Augustine of Hippo, St. *Confessions.* Translated by R. S. Pine-Coffin. London: Penguin Books Ltd., 1961. An excellent translation of Augustine's story of his conversion from hedonism to Christianity.

Dossey, Larry, M.D. *Healing Words: The Power of Prayer and the Practice of Medicine.* New York: Harper Collins, 1993. Anyone looking for scientific proof of the power of prayer will find that evidence in this book. Dossey writes from a medical perspective, not a religious one.

Keating, Thomas, O.C.S.O. *Open Mind, Open Heart.* Amity, N.Y.: Amity House, 1986. A useful guide for anyone who wants to learn more about contemplation and centering prayer.

Kelsey, Father Morton. *Healing and Christianity.* Minneapolis: Augsberg, 1995. A fascinating look at the history of Christian healing, from the time of Jesus up through the twentieth century. Helpful for understanding historically unhealthy attitudes about God and human suffering.

Lamott, Anne. *Traveling Mercies: Some Thoughts on Faith.* New York: Anchor Books, 1999. A personal, touching and often funny chronicle of one woman's faith journey, including her struggles with single-parenting.

Linn, Dennis and Matthew Linn. *Healing of Memories*. Mahwah, N.J.: Paulist Press, 1977. A basic book about inner healing. Includes discussion questions and exercises to help readers experience emotional healing and come to a deeper love of God, self, and others.

Linn, Dennis, Sheila Fabricant Linn, and Matthew Linn. *Don't Forgive Too Soon*. Mahwah, N.J.: Paulist Press, 1997. Through the use of stories, illustrations, and scripture, the Linns show that healthy forgiveness moves in stages. Chapters offer simple, healing processes for forgiveness.

Linn, Mary Jane, Dennis Linn, and Matthew Linn. *Healing the Dying*. Mahwah, N.J.: Paulist Press, 1979. Using the seven final acts and words of Jesus, the authors show what is needed in order to die as a healed and whole person. Chapters contain prayer suggestions and reflection questions. Recommended for those working with the dying, plus anyone willing to face his or her own issues surrounding death. Don't skip the preface.

MacNutt, Francis. *Healing*. Notre Dame, Ind.: Ave Maria Press, 1999. Based on practical experience, this is one of the clearest, most comprehensive books on the subject of religious healing.

Michael, Monsignor Chester P., and Marie C. Norrisey. *Prayer and Temperament: Different Prayer Forms for Different Personality Types*. Charlottesville, Va.: The Open Door, 1991. A prayer project involving hundreds of participants helped the authors discover which types of prayer work best for which personalities. Using the Myers-Briggs Type Indicator (e.g., introvert/extrovert), the book includes prayer suggestions for each personality type.

Normile, Patti. *Prayers for Care Givers*. Cincinnati, Ohio: St. Anthony Messenger Press, 1995. In the words of Leo Thomas, O.P., "The prayers in this astonishing book are cries from the heart from one who knows the rewards and the cost of caring for another."

Norris, Kathleen. *Amazing Grace: A Vocabulary of Faith*. New York: Riverhead Books, 1998. A poet's journey through language to faith, this book is indeed a source of amazing grace. The author's reflections on words such as fear, anger, God, Christian, and salvation bring them to life.

Nouwen, Henri J. M. *The Inner Voice of Love: A Journey Through Anguish to Freedom*. New York: Doubleday, 1996. Father Nouwen's "secret journal," written during a period of his life when he suddenly lost his self-esteem, his energy to live and work, and even his hope in God. Recommended for anyone living through the pain of broken relationships or the loss of a loved one.

Peck, M. Scott, M.D. *The Road Less Traveled*. New York: Simon & Schuster, 1978. A readable book with many case histories from Dr. Peck's psychiatric practice. It brings together psychological and spiritual insights and describes the process of becoming whole.

Remen, Rachel Naomi, M.D. *Kitchen Table Wisdom*. New York: Riverhead Books, 1996. Through the use of stories, this book looks at spiritual issues such as suffering, love, faith, and miracles. Very authentic because not only is the author a physician, a professor of medicine, and a therapist, but also she is a long-term survivor of a life-threatening chronic illness.

Rolheiser, Ronald, O.M.I. *The Holy Longing: A Search for Christian Spirituality*. New York: Doubleday, 1999. The author opens his preface by saying, "This is a book for you if you are struggling spiritually." How true.

Smedes, Lewis B. *The Art of Forgiving*. New York: Ballantine Books, 1997. A road map for those who are trying to make peace with a past hurt or betrayal. Through the use of examples, it leads readers through the three stages of for-giveness in order to arrive at inner peace.

Thomas, Leo, O.P., and Jan Alkire. *Formation for Healing Ministry*. Seattle: Institute for Christian Ministries, 2000. This is a spiritual formation program, not a book, designed for use in faith communities. More information can be found at www.healingministry.org.

Thomas, Leo, O.P., with Jan Alkire. *Healing Ministry: A Practical Guide*. Kansas City, Mo.: Sheed & Ward, 1994. For those who want to know how to reach out to others in life-giving ways. Reflection questions at the end of each chapter can also be used for one's own personal healing.

Thomas, Leo, O.P., and Jan Alkire. *Healing as a Parish Ministry*, 2nd ed. Seattle: Byron Books, 2000. (First ed.: Ave Maria Press, 1992). A practical guide for those who want to develop their ability to care for others and bring healing ministry into the normal life of a faith community.